The Tempo Implications
of
Bach's Notation

The Tempo Implications of Bach's Notation

IN THREE PARTS

Part 2—The Dance Suites

Leslie M. Kenney

WTB Press
Saunderstown, Rhode Island

WTB Press
PO Box 365, Saunderstown, RI 02874
WellTemperedBach.com

Copyright © Leslie M. Kenney 2021
All rights reserved. Published 2021

Cover Design: Anilda Carrasquillo, Cover to Cover Design
Cover Painting: *Go With the Flow* by Carmen Guedez, www.carmenguedez.com

Publisher's Cataloging-In-Publication Data
(Prepared by The Donohue Group, Inc.)

Names: Kenney, Leslie M., author.
Title: The tempo implications of Bach's notation. Part 2, The dance
    suites / Leslie M. Kenney.
Other Titles: Dance suites
Description: Saunderstown, Rhode Island : WTB Press, 2021. | "In three
    parts." | Includes bibliographical references and index.
Identifiers: ISBN 9781954699014 (paperback)
Subjects: LCSH: Bach, Johann Sebastian, 1685-1750--Criticism and
    interpretation. | Time in music--Mathematics. | Bach, Johann Se-
    bastian, 1685-1750. Instrumental music. Selections. | Instrumental
    music--Analysis, appreciation. | Dance music--Analysis, apprecia-
    tion.
Classification: LCC ML410.B13 K46 2021 MT6 | DDC 780.92 781.2/26--dc23

Library of Congress Control Number: 2021909024

Contents

	Abbreviations	vi

Part Two   **The Dance Suites**

	Introduction	3
Seven	Introductory Movements	8
Eight	Allemandes and Allemandas	22
Nine	Courantes and Correntes	34
Ten	Sarabandes	49
Eleven	Gigas and Gigues	62
Twelve	Movements with Other Titles	75
	Appendix—Overview of Bach's Dance Music	93
	Bibliography	97
	Index of Cited Works	99

Abbreviations

Am. B. *Amalien Bibliothek*, the Duchess Anna Amalia Library in Weimar, Germany

BG *Bach Gesellschaft* (Bach Society), formed in 1850 to publish the complete Bach works

BWV *Bach-Werke-Verzeichnis* (Bach Works Catalog), published by Wolfgang Schmieder in 1950

CS *Cello Suite*

ES *English Suite*

Fas Faszikel [fascicle, or bundle, in English]

FO *French Overture*

FS *French Suite*

KP *Keyboard Partita*

LS *Lute Suite*

m Measure

mm Measures

NBA *Neue Bach Ausgabe* (New Bach Edition), the second complete edition of the music of Johann Sebastian Bach, published between 1954 and 2007 by Bärenreiter

OED *The Oxford English Dictionary*

P Partitur (score)

St Stimmen (parts)

VP *Violin Partita*

2

The Dance Suites

La Camargo Dancing
Detail from a 1730 Oil Painting by Nicolas Lancret
of Marie-Anne de Culpas de Camargo (1710–1770)

Introduction

Dancing played a prominent role in seventeenth-century Europe. One reason it was so prominent was because of the renowned dancing skills of Louis XIV of France (1638–1715), the most powerful king in Europe. Known as the "Sun King," Louis structured his court life to showcase his dancing. In order to emulate Louis's court, German states often hired French dancing masters, preferably Parisian. Like most citizens of German states, Bach was exposed to French culture from childhood. In Bach's obituary, his son C. P. E. Bach (1714–1788) and his student Johann Friedrich Agricola (1720–1774) write,

> From Lüneburg[1] he journeyed now and again to Hamburg . . . to go and listen to a then-famous band kept by the Duke of Celle, consisting for the most part of Frenchmen; thus he acquired a thorough grounding in the French taste, which, in those regions, was at the time something quite new.[2]

The music that was used to accompany dancing became so popular that instrumentalists performed it for its own sake, resulting in the development of sets of dance pieces called *suites*. The term *suite* (from the French word meaning "those that follow" or "succession") did not come into use until the last quarter of the seventeenth century.[3] The groups of dances to which the term was eventually applied evolved from pairs of fourteenth-century dances.[4] The first dance of a pair was slow, with elegant, gliding steps, and was usually in duple meter. The second was fast, with skips, hops, and leaps, and was usually in triple meter. The melodic and harmonic materials of the first dance were often used again in the second. In the fifteenth century, the first dance was often titled Basse Danse (Bassadanza in Italian) and the second Saltarello.[5] In the sixteenth and seventeenth centuries, the first dance was often titled either Pavane (Pavana in Italian) or Passamezzo, and the second was often titled either Saltarello or Gagliarda.[6]

The sets of dances that appear around the beginning of the seventeenth century were most often composed for lute. These dances were grouped by key (to avoid the need to retune the instrument between movements) but did not share thematic material. In 1611 the lutenist Paul Peuerl (c. 1570–after 1625) published ten sets of four dances, all using

---

1 Bach lived in Lüneburg between 1700 and 1703.
2 David and Mendel, eds., *New Bach Reader*, 300.
3 Other terms for the suite include *suite de danses*, *partita*, and *ordre*.
4 David Fuller, "Suite," *The New Grove Dictionary*, xxiv, 668.
5 The title Basse Danse means "low dance" and refers to the dance's gliding steps, where the dancers keep their feet on the ground (or "low"). The title Saltarello derives from the Italian verb *saltare* ("to jump") and refers to the dance's frequent leaps.
6 Randel, ed., *The Harvard Dictionary*, 340, 639–40.

the order Paduana-Intrada-Dantz-Gagliarda, each set making a coherent musical whole. Sets in the order Allemande-Courante-Sarabande appeared in French lute music around 1630. German harpsichordists added the gigue around 1665 and standardized the order as Allemande-Courante-Sarabande-Gigue.[7] For Bach, these became the four core movements of the suite.

The Englishman Thomas Mace (c. 1613–1709), in 1676, was the first writer to describe the suite (or "suit") as a conventional order of pieces,[8]

> I will *now* set you a Sett, or a *Suit of Lessons*, (as we commonly call *Them*) which may be of any *Number*, as you please, yet commonly are about *Half a Dozen*.
>
> The First always, should begin, in the Nature of a *Voluntary Play*, which we call a *Praeludium*, or a *Prelude*.
>
> Then, *Allmaine, Ayre, Coranto, Seraband, Toy* or what you please, provided They be all in the *same Key*; yet (in my opinion) in regard we call Them a *Suit of Lessons*, They ought to be something of a Kin, (as we use to say) or to have some kind of *Resemblance in their Conceits, Natures, or Humours*.[9]

Suites consistently include movements in addition to the four core movements. As Mace states, many include an introductory movement, usually titled Prelude. Most suites include additional movements later in the suite (as do all of Bach's). Such movements were usually inserted between the sarabande and the gigue and are often termed *galanteries* today.

Bach's Suites

We select thirty Bach suites[10] for examination and refer to them by abbreviations. When the suite is part of a set, the abbreviation is followed by a number that indicates the position of the suite within the set. For example, the abbreviation ES1 represents *English Suite 1* and CS2 represents *Cello Suite 2*. Table II.1 lists these suites, along with their BWV numbers and abbreviations, the number of suites in each set, the approximate date(s) of composition, and the library catalog number for the most authoritative source(s). Page vi gives the meaning of other abbreviations used in this table.

With the possible exception of *Lute Suite 1*, the *English Suites* are the earliest written and thus probably represent a prototype for later suites. Affording them special attention establishes stylistic and notational norms, leading to greater appreciation for Bach's later deviations from tradition.

---

7   Randel, ed., *The Harvard Dictionary*, 848.
8   David Fuller, "Suite," *The New Grove Dictionary*, xxiv, 665.
9   Mace, *Musick's Monument*, 120.
10 We exclude the four *Orchestral Suites* (BWV 1066–1069) from our discussion because the original sources disagree on the time signature for numerous movements, making it problematic to use them to determine the tempo implications of Bach's dance titles.

TABLE II.1 The thirty suites in our study, along with their BWV numbers and abbreviations, the number of suites in each set, the approximate date(s) of composition (taken from *The New Grove Dictionary*), and the library catalog number for the most authoritative source(s), ordered by BWV number

Name of Set	BWV Number	Abbreviation	Number of Suites in the Set	Approximate Date(s) of Composition	Library Catalog Number for Most Authoritative Sources
English Suites	806–811	ES	6	before 1720	P 1072, Fas. 2
French Suites	812–817	FS	6	1722–1725	P 224, P 225, P 418 & P 420
Keyboard Partitas	825–830	KP	6	1726–1731	Mus. 2405-T-46
French Overture	831	FO	1	1735	Am. B. 64
Lute Suites	996, 997	LS	2	1710–1717 & 1738–1741	P 801 & P 650
Violin Partitas	1002, 1004, 1006	VP	3	1720	P 967
Cello Suites	1007–1012	CS	6	c. 1720	P 269
Total number of suites			30		

Description of the Authoritative Sources

- The *English Suites* survive in the handwriting of Bach's student and copyist Bernhard Christian Kayser (P 1072, Faszikel 2).
- An autograph score survives for a portion of the *French Suites* (P 224). Most of the remainder survives in the handwriting of either Bach's second wife Anna Magdalena Bach (P 225) or of his students Bernhard Christian Kayser (P 418) and Johann Caspar Vogler (P 420).
- The *Keyboard Partitas* and the *French Overture* were published during Bach's lifetime (e.g., Mus. 2405-T-46 and Am. B. 64).
- *Lute Suite 1* survives in the handwriting of Bach's cousin Johann Gottfried Walther (P 801). *Lute Suite 2* survives in the handwriting of Bach's student and copyist Johann Friedrich Agricola (P 650).
- An autograph score survives for the *Violin Partitas* (P 967).
- The *Cello Suites* survive in the handwriting of Anna Magdalena Bach (P 269).

Important Note: In an earlier work (*The Proportional Method*) we set forth the logic that is the basis for understanding the tempo implications of Bach's notation. It is essential that the reader be familiar with our results, a summary of which we present below. The reader is encouraged to study all of *The Proportional Method* for a full understanding of the thinking that led to these results.

Summary of Bach's Proportional Method

There are two fixed pulse rates that we refer to as the normal tactus (72 BPM) and the accelerated tactus (81 BPM). The speed of the shortest note value of a movement is a multiple of the speed of the tactus. The size of the multiple depends on the shortest note value itself, disregarding ornamental notes (table II.2).

TABLE II.2 The number of shortest notes per tactus ranges from two to eight

Shortest Note Value	Number of Shortest Notes per Tactus
𝅘𝅥𝅱	8
𝅘𝅥𝅰	6
𝅘𝅥𝅯	4
♪	3
♩	2

The time signatures **C**, **¢**, **𝇋**, **2**, and **𝟤̸** tell the musician which tactus speed to use. Those without a stroke (**C** and **2**) specify the normal tactus, while those with a stroke (**¢**, **𝇋**, and **𝟤̸**) specify the accelerated tactus. In addition, the signatures **𝇋**, **2**, and **𝟤̸** increase the number of shortest notes per tactus. When a work begins with a double-integer numeric time signature such as $\frac{3}{4}$, it uses the normal tactus. Double-integer signatures that appear later in a work continue to use the tactus of the immediately preceding music.

All of Bach's rarely used Italian performance markings describe his intended musical effect. In some movements with performance markings, but not in all of them:

- The markings *Alla breve*, *Allegro*, *Presto*, and *Vivace* instruct the musician to use the next larger number of shortest notes per tactus.
- The markings *Adagio*, *Andante*, and *Largo* instruct the musician to use the next smaller number of shortest notes per tactus.

Organization of the Material

The thirty suites in our study include 205 movements, as shown in table II.3. Separate chapters are devoted to introductory movements, allemandes, courantes, sarabandes, gigues, and movements with other titles.

TABLE II.3 The type and number of movements examined in each chapter

Chapter	Type of Movement	Number of Movements
1	Introductory Movements	22
2	Allemandes & Allemandas	27
3	Courantes & Correntes	29
4	Sarabandes	29
5	Gigas & Gigues	28
6	Movements with Other Titles	70
Total number of movements		205

Tempo implications are usually clear. However, because Bach often fully notated the pitches and rhythms of ornamentation, the musician must differentiate between ornamental notes and non-ornamental notes when determining the note value used to set tempo (non-ornamental notes are also called essential notes).[11] In addition, many of Bach's dances, including allemandes, courantes, sarabandes, and gigues, derive from long-established traditions, so their titles may contain clues concerning tempo. In cases where ambiguities exist, Bach's proportional method yields only two, clearly contrasting, tempos. By considering all the movements of each dance type as a group, and by referring to contemporaneous descriptions of that type, we are able to decide between the alternative tempos.

We structure each chapter as follows:

- First, we investigate the origins of the movement type.
- Next, we review the contemporaneous performance practice literature.
- Then, we examine the notation of each movement to discover what the tempo would be according to the proportional method.
- Last, we consider what tempo information, if any, Bach's dance titles provide.

---

11 Kenney, *Proportional Method*, 14–15.

7
Introductory Movements

While eight suites begin with an allemande, the remaining twenty-two begin with an introductory movement that is not a dance. The title Prelude[1] occurs sixteen times, Overture[2] twice, and Fantasia, Praeambulum, Sinfonia, and Toccata one time each.

The word *prelude* derives from the Latin word *praeludere*, whose prefix *prae-* means "before" and whose root *ludere* means "to play." The German translation is *Praeludium*, the Italian is *preludio*, and the French is *prélude*. The title Prelude originally indicated an improvisation that allowed the performer to warm up, check tuning, establish tonality, and attract audience attention.[3] Jean-Jacques Rousseau (1712–1778), the Genevan philosopher and composer, defines the verb *to prelude* in 1768,

> To sing or play some stroke of irregular fantasy, rather short, but passing by the essential chords of the [key], either to establish or to dispose the voice, or to place the hand well on an instrument before the beginning of a piece of music.[4]

The title Overture derives from the French word *ouverture*, which in the seventeenth century denoted a piece of music introducing a ballet, opera, or oratorio. (Alternatively, such movements were sometimes titled Sinfonia or Introduzione.[5]) The meaning of *ouverture* ("opening" in English) refers to the practice of opening the theater curtain toward the end of the movement. Bach followed the French overture model, which was established by Louis XIV's court composer, Jean-Baptiste de Lully (1632–1687). The first section is homophonic, with a slow tempo, sharply dotted rhythms, and elaborate ornamentation, while the second section is polyphonic, with a faster tempo and consistent motion of the shortest note value. The second section is sometimes followed by a shortened restatement of the first section.[6] Bach never used the Italian overture model, which had three homophonic sections in the order fast-slow-fast.

Table 7.1 gives the number of introductory movements in each of Bach's sets of suites. While most introductory movements have a single section, four have two sections, and one has three.

---

1 Or Praeludium, Praeludio, or Preludio.
2 Or Ouverture.
3 David Ledbetter, "Prelude," *The New Grove Dictionary*, xx, 291.
4 Rousseau, *A Complete Dictionary of Music*, 323.
5 Randel, ed., *The Harvard Dictionary*, 625.
6 Nicholas Temperly, "Overture," *The New Grove Dictionary*, xviii, 824.

TABLE 7.1 The seven sets of suites in our study, the number of introductory movements in each set, the introductory movements that have more than one section, and the suites that lack introductory movements

Name of Work	Number of Introductory Movements	Introductory Movements That Have More Than One Section	Suites That Lack Introductory Movements
English Suites	6		
French Suites			FS1–FS6
Keyboard Partitas	6	KP2, KP4	
French Overture	1	FO	
Lute Suites	2	LS1	
Violin Partitas	1		VP1, VP2
Cello Suites	6	CS5	
Total	22		

Thesis of This Chapter

Because introductory movements derive from improvisation, their titles can have no tempo-related meaning.

The English Suite Preludes

The ES1 prelude (ex. 7.1) uses the time signature $\frac{12}{8}$, the normal tactus,[7] the dotted quarter as beat note, and, after the first two measures, the eighth as shortest note. The sixteenth notes in the first two measures must be considered ornamental because if they were

EXAMPLE 7.1 Prelude from *English Suite 1* (BWV 806/1); mm. 1–5

---

[7] Because this prelude is the initial movement of the work, and because it uses a double-integer-numeric time signature, it uses the normal tactus, as discussed in *The Proportional Method* (pages 30–32).

essential the tempo would be a lethargic 48 BPM.[8] Thus, we should consider the sixteenth notes in measures 1 and 2 as an ornamental flourish that establishes the key and introduces a gentle, pastoral, musical effect. The tempo is 72 BPM.[9]

The other five ES preludes are also single-section movements, with ES2 and ES4 in simple meter and ES3, ES5, and ES6 in compound meter. The tempo for the ES2 prelude is 72 BPM[10] because the signature is $\frac{3}{4}$, the tactus is normal, the beat note is the quarter, and the shortest note is the sixteenth (ex. 7.2A).

EXAMPLE 7.2 The two *English Suite* preludes where the meter is simple

Note: The above scan from the *Bach Gesellschaft* of the *English Suite 4* prelude has been adjusted to show the signature ₵ for reasons presented in the text.

The earliest surviving manuscript of the ES4 prelude (ex. 7.2B, above), in the handwriting of Bach's student and copyist Bernhard Christian Kayser (1705–1758), shows the time signature ₵.[11] While the *Neue Bach Ausgabe* (NBA) also shows ₵, the *Bach Gesellschaft* (BG) shows **C**. We accept the time signature as ₵ because the earliest source and recent scholarship agree, so the tactus is accelerated. The shortest note is the sixteenth, and, because of the harmonic rhythm, the beat note is the quarter. The tempo is 81 BPM.[12]

The tempo for the ES3 and ES5 preludes is 48 BPM[13] because the tactus is normal, the shortest note is the sixteenth, and the beat note is the dotted quarter (ex. 7.3A and B). Although the prelude's origins are based in improvisation, all of Bach's preludes employ contrapuntal techniques such as imitation. These two preludes in particular employ strict fugal writing and are not perceived as improvisational.

---

8   4 sixteenth notes per tactus x 72 BPM ÷ 6 sixteenth notes per dotted quarter note.
9   3 eighth notes per tactus x 72 BPM ÷ 3 eighth notes per dotted quarter note.
10 4 sixteenth notes per tactus x 72 BPM ÷ 4 sixteenth notes per quarter note.
11 Library Catalog Number: P 1072, Faszikel 2.
12 81 BPM replaces 72 BPM as the tactus speed.
13 4 sixteenth notes per tactus x 72 BPM ÷ 6 sixteenth notes per dotted quarter note.

EXAMPLE 7.3 The preludes from *English Suite 3* and *English Suite 5*

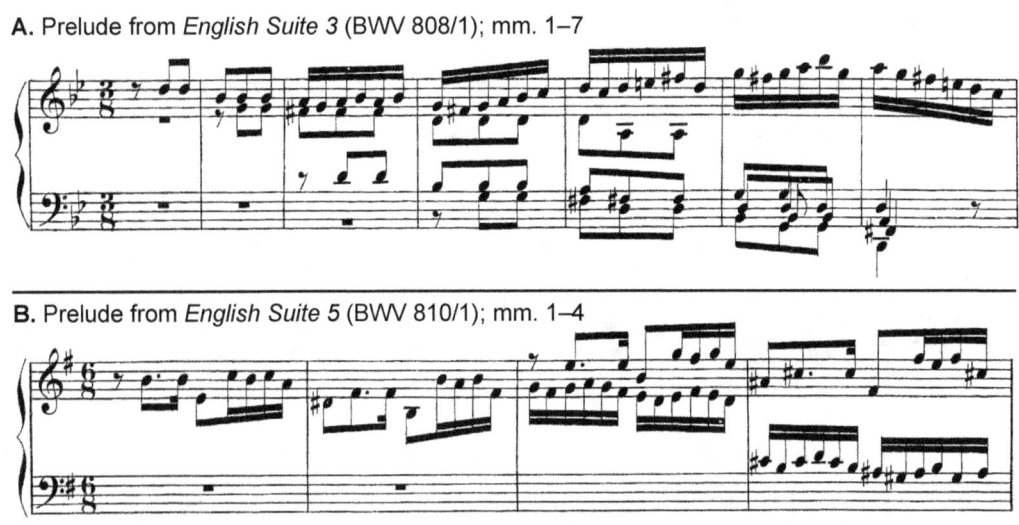

A. Prelude from *English Suite 3* (BWV 808/1); mm. 1–7

B. Prelude from *English Suite 5* (BWV 810/1); mm. 1–4

The ES6 prelude deserves special attention because its two substantial passages are separated by a measure marked *Adagio*. Throughout the movement, the time signature is $\frac{9}{8}$ and the tactus is normal (ex. 7.4). The tempo for the thirty-six-measure passage that precedes the *Adagio* is 72 BPM[14] because the shortest note is the eighth (the numerous sixteenth notes appearing later in this passage are clearly ornamental).

EXAMPLE 7.4 Prelude from *English Suite 6* (BWV 811/1); the opening measures of the first half

The *Adagio* in measure 37 interrupts the forward motion of the earlier section (ex. 7.5, following page) and is an invitation to improvise rather than a tempo instruction. Measure 38 begins the 158-measure-long *Allegro*, where the shortest note is the sixteenth rather than the eighth. As discussed in our earlier work, all of Bach's rarely used Italian performance markings describe his intended musical effect. Many of these markings, but not all of them, also alter the number of shortest notes per tactus.[15] Here, the marking *Allegro* must increase the number of shortest notes per tactus from four to six because if it did not the tempo

---

14   3 eighth notes per tactus x 72 BPM ÷ 3 eighth notes per dotted quarter note.
15   Kenney, *Proportional Method*, 51–52.

for this passage would be a too slow 48 BPM.[16] Thus, the tempo is the same as that of the opening passage (72 BPM).[17]

EXAMPLE 7.5 Prelude from *English Suite 6* (BWV 811/1); measure 37, marked *Adagio*, acts as a transition to the *Allegro*, which begins in measure 38; mm. 36–39

The opening has a gentle, pastoral quality, while the extended *Allegro* is virtuosic and exciting. While they are related by having the same meter and tempo, their differing musical effects foreshadow the structure of the later preludes that have truly independent sections.

Later-Composed Single-Section Introductory Movements

After the *English Suite* preludes, Bach wrote eleven single-section introductory movements, shown in table 7.2.

TABLE 7.2 The eleven single-section introductory movements (other than those in the *English Suites*), grouped by shortest note, tactus speed, and meter type

Shortest Note	Tactus Speed	Simple Meter	Compound Meter
♪	Normal	KP5, VP3, CS1, CS3	
♪	Accelerated	LS2, CS2, CS4	KP3, CS6
♬	Normal	KP1	
♬	Accelerated	KP6	

The preludes from KP5, VP3, CS1, and CS3 all use simple meter, the normal tactus, and the sixteenth as shortest note (ex. 7.6). The resulting proportional tempo is 72 BPM.[18] These pieces are examples of moderate-tempo Bach movements that today's performers tend to play much faster than the proportional tempo. Playing them at the proportional tempo requires accurate rhythm, crisp articulation, and intelligently conceived phrasing and results in charming musical effects in accord with contemporaneous descriptions.

---

16 4 sixteenth notes per tactus x 72 BPM ÷ 6 sixteenth notes per dotted quarter note.
17 6 replaces 4 as the number of sixteenth notes per tactus.
18 4 sixteenth notes per tactus x 72 BPM ÷ 4 sixteenth notes per quarter note.

EXAMPLE 7.6 The four introductory movements where the meter is simple, the tactus is normal, and the shortest note is the sixteenth

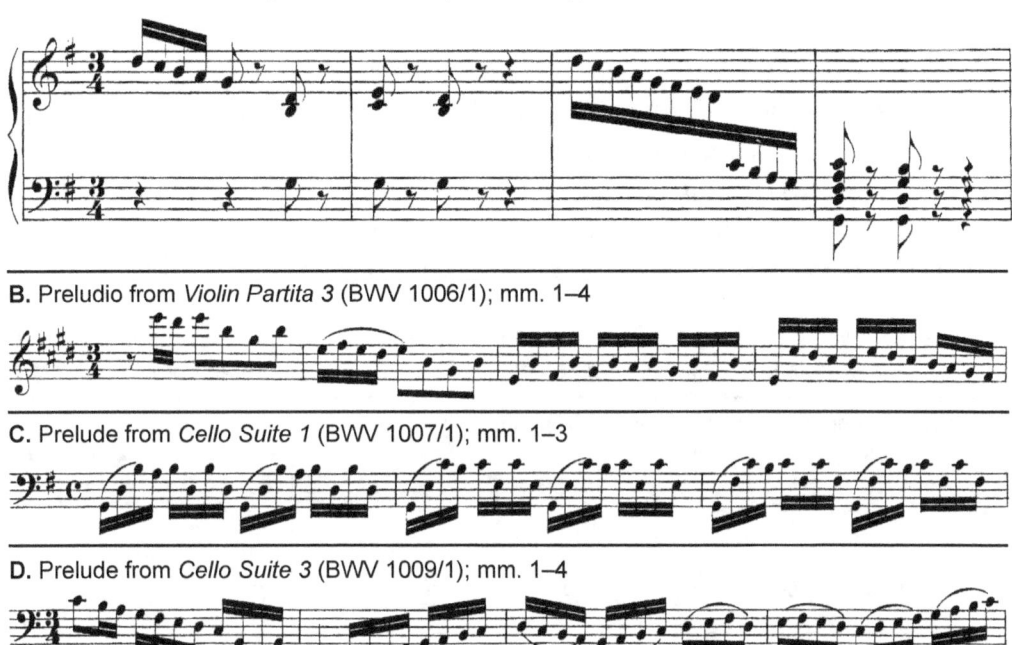

A. Praeambulum from *Keyboard Partita 5* (BWV 829/1); mm. 1–4

B. Preludio from *Violin Partita 3* (BWV 1006/1); mm. 1–4

C. Prelude from *Cello Suite 1* (BWV 1007/1); mm. 1–3

D. Prelude from *Cello Suite 3* (BWV 1009/1); mm. 1–4

The music of the VP3 preludio occurs in two other works: the sinfonia that introduces the second half of *Cantata 120a* and the opening movement of *Cantata 29*. Bach probably had a single tempo in mind for all three versions, so these cantata movements may shed light on the tempo of the VP3 preludio itself.

The organ part for the *Cantata 120a* sinfonia (composed in 1728 or 1729) closely follows the VP3 preludio. None of the original parts[19] for *Cantata 120a* include a performance marking, and the autograph score is no longer extant. Bach reused the *Cantata 120a* sinfonia as the opening movement of *Cantata 29*, which he composed for the 1731 Leipzig town council inauguration. The autograph score of this cantata,[20] reproduced in facsimile in the BG,[21] clearly lacks a performance marking. Eighteen of the nineteen surviving original parts also lack a marking but the original organ part[22] shows *Presto*. This marking is included in both the BG and the NBA. If *Presto* were to increase the number of shortest notes per tactus, then the tempo would be 108 BPM.[23] A performance at 108 BPM would lack the charm of a performance at a less ostentatious tempo, and it would obscure the counterpoint. We conclude that *Presto* does not increase the number of shortest notes per tactus, so the tempo for the sinfonias in both cantatas is 72 BPM, the same tempo as for the preludio.

---

19 Library Catalog Number: St 43.
20 Library Catalog Number: P 166.
21 *Bach Gesellschaft*, xliv, 84.
22 Library Catalog Number: St 106.
23 6 replaces 4 as the number of sixteenth notes per tactus.

The LS2 and CS4 preludes use simple meter and have the sixteenth as shortest note. We find the following evidence that both use the accelerated tactus:

- A score in the handwriting of Johann Friedrich Agricola[24] shows ¢ for LS2 (ex. 7.7A). Because this is the earliest source, we accept ¢, even though both the BG and the NBA show C.
- A score in the handwriting of Anna Magdalena Bach[25] and also the NBA show ¢ for CS4 (ex. 7.7B). The BG shows C. We accept ¢ because the earliest source and recent scholarship agree.

Because these two movements have the sixteenth as shortest note and the quarter as beat note, and because they use the accelerated tactus, their tempo is 81 BPM.[26]

EXAMPLE 7.7 Two introductory movements where the meter is simple, the tactus is accelerated, and the shortest note is the sixteenth; sixteenths appear later in the prelude from *Cello Suite 4*

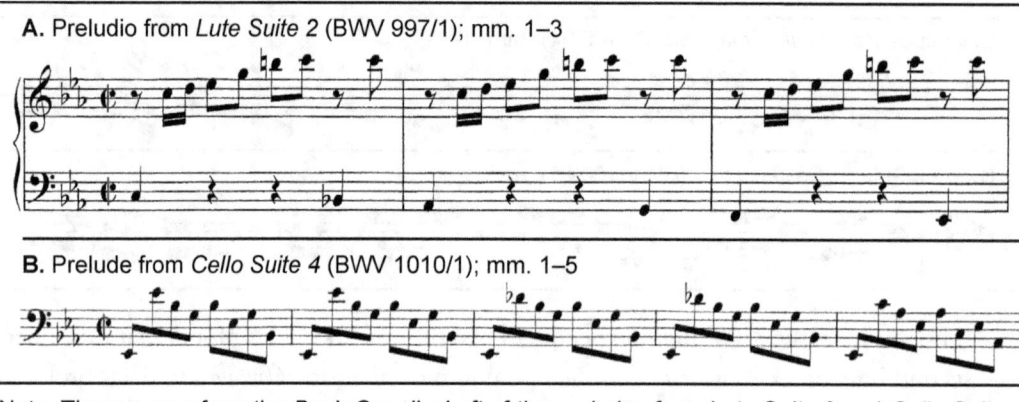

Note: These scans from the *Bach Gesellschaft* of the preludes from *Lute Suite 2* and *Cello Suite 4* have been adjusted to show the signature ¢ for reasons presented in the text.

The KP3, CS2, and CS6 preludes (ex. 7.8) use numeric time signatures ($\frac{3}{8}$, $\frac{3}{4}$, and $\frac{12}{8}$, respectively). As we saw in *The Proportional Method*, movements using numeric time signatures continue to use the tactus of the preceding movement, unless they are the opening movement of a work.[27] Regarding Bach's sets of dance suites, is each suite considered a "work," or is it only the whole set that is considered a "work?"

- If each suite is considered a "work," then these three movements would use the normal tactus.
- If the individual suites are considered parts of the whole set, then their preludes would continue to use the accelerated tactus established in the preceding suites, unaltered by any subsequent mensural signature.[28]

---

24 Library Catalog Number: P 650.
25 Library Catalog Number: P 269.
26 4 sixteenth notes per tactus x 81 BPM ÷ 4 sixteenth notes per quarter note.
27 Kenney, *Proportional Method*, 30–32.
28 The CS6 prelude would adopt the accelerated tactus from the two-movement earlier CS5 gavotte, while the CS2 prelude and KP3 fantasia would adopt the accelerated tactus from the CS1 and KP2 allemandes, respectively.

EXAMPLE 7.8 Three introductory movements that use a numeric time signature

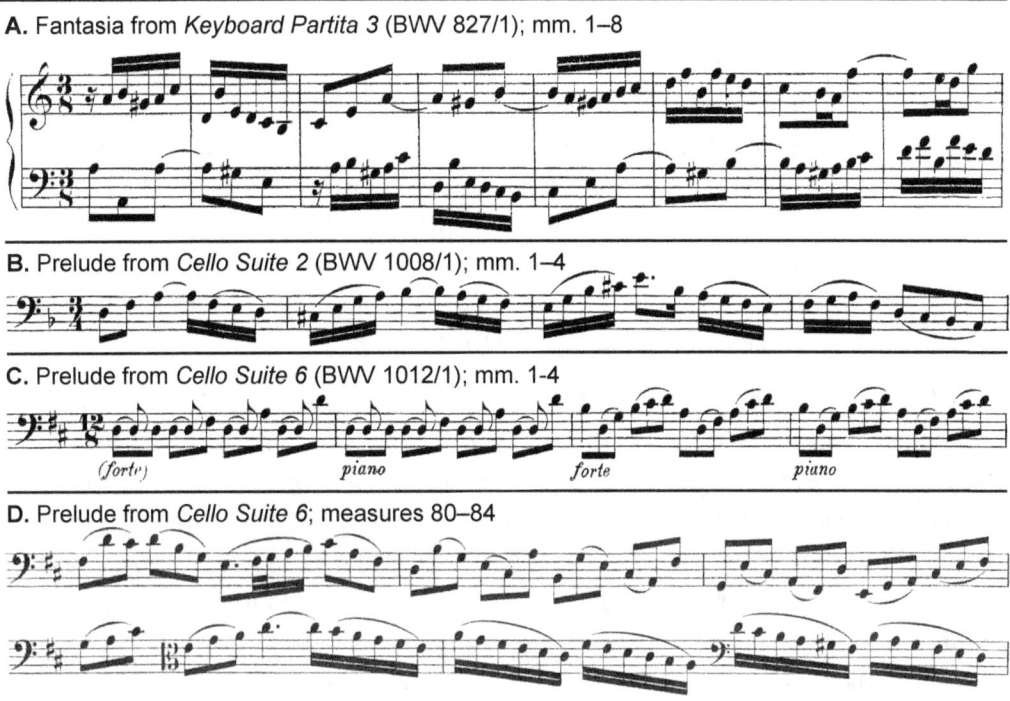

A. Fantasia from *Keyboard Partita 3* (BWV 827/1); mm. 1–8

B. Prelude from *Cello Suite 2* (BWV 1008/1); mm. 1–4

C. Prelude from *Cello Suite 6* (BWV 1012/1); mm. 1–4

D. Prelude from *Cello Suite 6*; measures 80–84

It may not be possible to determine definitively whether a whole set or a single movement constitutes a work, both because of the limited sample size[29] and because the alternative tempos differ by only one-eighth. We invite readers to try the normal-tactus and accelerated-tactus tempos for these movements to see if they concur with the author in preferring the accelerated-tactus tempos:

- The KP3 fantasia (ex. 7.8A, above) uses compound meter and has the sixteenth as shortest note, so its normal-tactus tempo would be 48 BPM,[30] while its accelerated-tactus tempo would be 54 BPM.[31] A fantasia is "an ingenious and imaginative instrumental composition, often characterized by its departure from current stylistic and structural norms."[32] Perhaps Bach titled this movement Fantasia because of its syncopations and because of the theme's frequent changes in melodic direction.
- The CS2 prelude (ex. 7.8B, also above) uses simple meter and has the sixteenth as shortest note, so its normal-tactus tempo would be 72 BPM,[33] while its accelerated-tactus tempo would be 81 BPM.[34] This prelude is an example of a moderate-tempo Bach movement that today's performers tend to play much slower than

---

29 The only other movements to consider would be the opening movements of *Clavier Übung, Part 2*, which may adopt the accelerated tactus from the final movement of *Clavier Übung, Part 1*.
30 4 sixteenth notes per tactus x 72 BPM ÷ 6 sixteenth notes per dotted quarter note.
31 81 BPM replaces 72 BPM as the tactus speed.
32 Randel, ed., *The Harvard Dictionary*, 307.
33 4 sixteenth notes per tactus x 72 BPM ÷ 4 sixteenth notes per quarter note.
34 81 BPM replaces 72 BPM as the tactus speed.

the proportional tempo. Playing it at the proportional tempo requires establishing only one beat per measure rather than three. It also requires a light touch and an improvisational flair.

- The CS6 prelude uses the time signature $\frac{12}{8}$. For most of the movement, including the first seventy-seven measures, the shortest note is the eighth (ex. 7.8C, preceding page). However, sixteenth notes, and even a few thirty-second notes, appear in brief passages, such as measures 80–84 (ex. 7.8D, also preceding page). The thirty-second notes are clearly ornamental, so the sixteenth is the shortest essential note value, and the prelude's normal-tactus tempo would be 48 BPM,[35] while its accelerated-tactus tempo would be 54 BPM.[36]

The KP1 praeludium (ex. 7.9A) and the KP6 toccata (ex. 7.9B) use the quarter as beat note and the thirty-second as shortest note. The tempo for the KP1 praeludium is 54 BPM[37] because its time signature is **C**, which specifies the normal tactus. The tempo for the KP6 toccata is 61 BPM[38] because its time signature is ¢, which specifies the accelerated tactus. A "toccata" is "a virtuoso composition for keyboard or plucked string instrument featuring sections of brilliant passage work."[39] Measure 3 and fourteen other measures of this movement fill each beat with seven sixteenth notes. This unusual rhythmic feature occurs in no other Bach movement and produces both brilliant passage work and a feeling of improvisation.

EXAMPLE 7.9 The two introductory movements where the shortest note is the thirty-second

A. Praeludium from *Keyboard Partita 1* (BWV 825/1) uses the time signature **C**; mm. 1–2

B. Toccata from *Keyboard Partita 6* (BWV 830/1) uses the time signature ¢; mm. 1–3

---

35   4 sixteenth notes per tactus x 72 BPM ÷ 6 sixteenth notes per dotted quarter note.
36   81 BPM replaces 72 BPM as the tactus speed.
37   6 thirty-second notes per tactus x 72 BPM ÷ 8 thirty-second notes per quarter note.
38   81 BPM replaces 72 BPM as the tactus speed.
39   Randel, ed., *The Harvard Dictionary*, 895.

Multi-Section Introductory Movements

Of the five multi-section introductory movements, two are titled Overture (KP4 and FO), two are titled Prelude (CS5 and LS1), and one is titled Sinfonia (KP2). All five exhibit aspects of the French overture, with a slow, homophonic first section using dotted rhythms and a fast, polyphonic final section using consistent motion of the shortest note value. Because the KP4, FO, and CS5 introductory movements have identical features, they use the same two tempos:

- The first sections (and the return to the first section in FO) have the tempo 61 BPM[40] because the beat note is the quarter, the shortest note is the thirty-second, and the time signature ¢ specifies the accelerated tactus (ex. 7.10A, ex. 7.11A, and ex. 7.12A).
- The second sections have the tempo 54 BPM[41] because the beat note is the dotted quarter, the shortest note is the sixteenth, and the tactus is accelerated,[42] (ex. 7.10B, ex. 7.11B, and ex. 7.12B).

EXAMPLE 7.10 Ouverture from *Keyboard Partita 4* (BWV 828/1)

A. The beginning of the first section

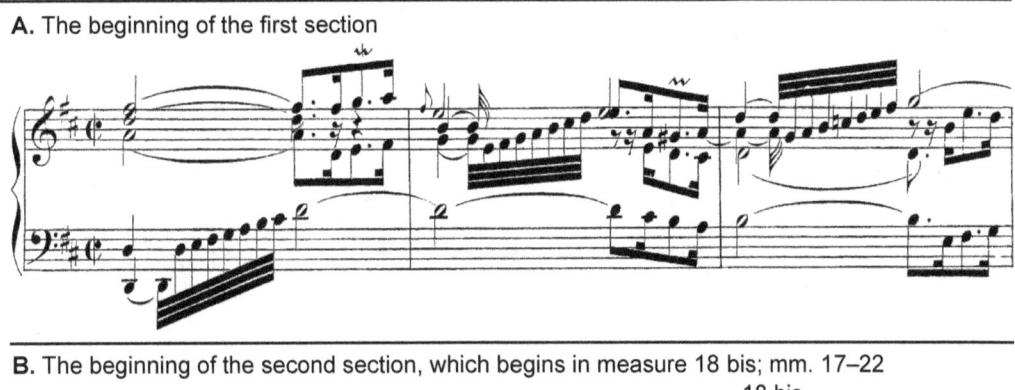

B. The beginning of the second section, which begins in measure 18 bis; mm. 17–22

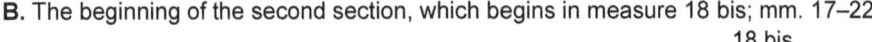
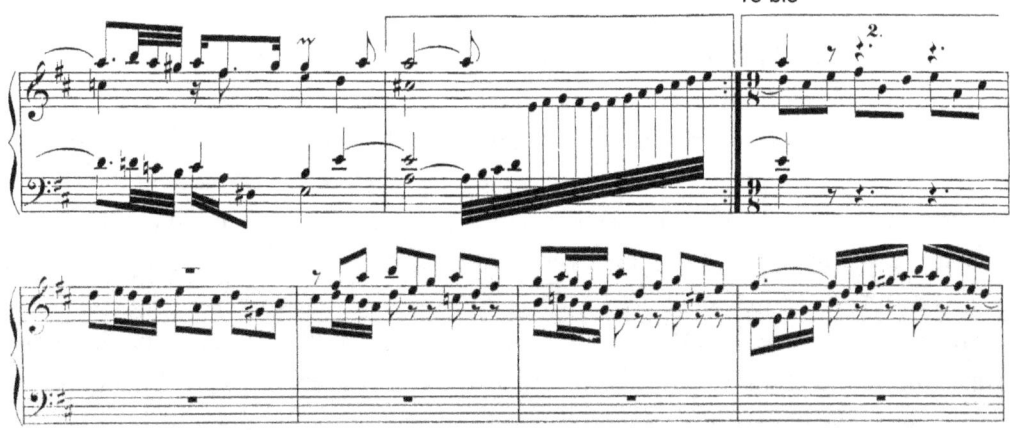

---

40 6 thirty-second notes per tactus x 81 BPM ÷ 8 thirty-second notes per quarter note.
41 4 sixteenth notes per tactus x 81 BPM ÷ 6 sixteenth notes per dotted quarter note.
42 The accelerated tactus is adopted from each movement's first section.

EXAMPLE 7.11 The first movement of the *French Overture* (BWV 831/1)

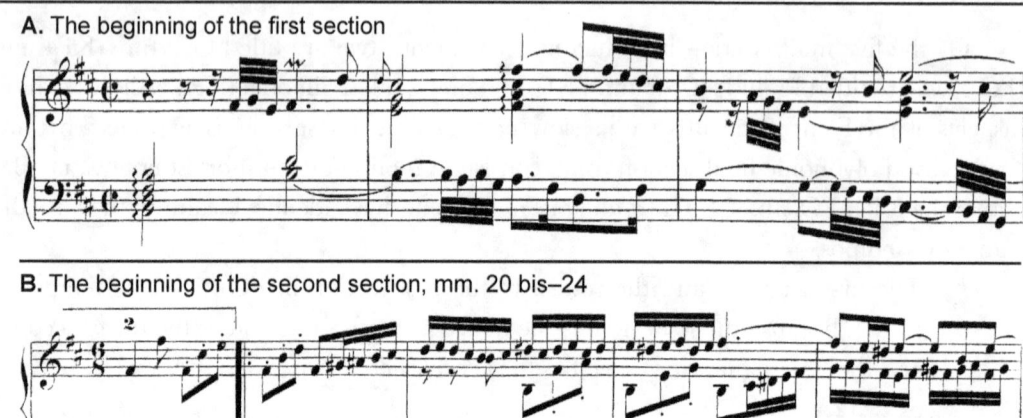

A. The beginning of the first section

B. The beginning of the second section; mm. 20 bis–24

EXAMPLE 7.12 Prelude from *Cello Suite 5* (BWV 1011/1)

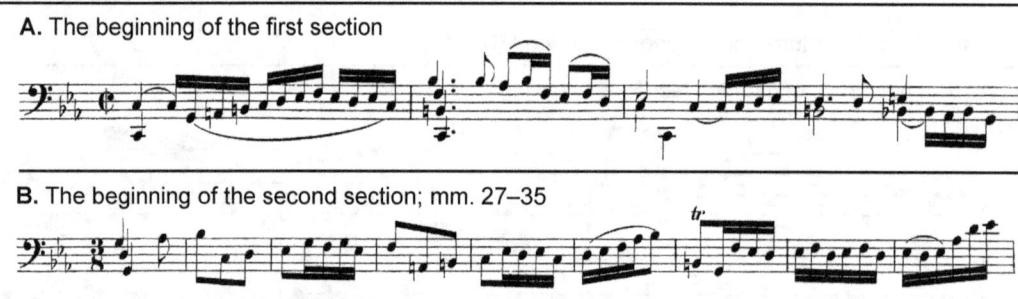

A. The beginning of the first section

B. The beginning of the second section; mm. 27–35

Note: This scan from the *Bach Gesellschaft* of the *Cello Suite 5* prelude has been adjusted to show the signature ¢ for reasons presented in the text.

A score in the handwriting of Anna Magdalena Bach[43] and the NBA both show ¢ for the CS5 prelude (ex. 7.12A, above). The BG shows C. We accept ¢ because the earliest source and recent scholarship agree.

The tempo for the first section of the LS1 praeludio (ex. 7.13A) is 54 BPM[44] because the time signature is C, there is no performance marking, and the shortest essential note is the thirty-second (thirty-second notes and a few clearly ornamental sixty-fourth notes appear later). The second section uses the signature $\frac{3}{8}$, the normal tactus, and the sixteenth as shortest note (ex. 7.13B). This section is marked *Presto* in the BG and the NBA, both of which rely on three extant eighteenth-century manuscripts, none an autograph. The marking *Presto* appears in the earliest source, which is a copy by Bach's cousin Johann Gottfried Walther, made between 1710–1717.[45] A copy from the 1720s by Bach's pupil Heinrich Nikolaus Gerber shows no marking.[46] Another eighteenth-century copy by an unknown

---

43 Library Catalog Number: P 269.
44 6 thirty-second notes per tactus x 72 BPM ÷ 8 thirty-second notes per quarter note.
45 Library Catalog Number: P 801, Faszikel 22.
46 Library Catalog Number: MS 10149.

scribe has not been accessible to the author.[47] However, the NBA *Kritischer Bericht* indicates that this copy also lacks the marking.[48] Thus, the manuscript evidence, although weighted toward the lack of a marking, is inconclusive.

EXAMPLE 7.13 Praeludio from *Lute Suite 1* (BWV 996/1)

A. The beginning of the first section

B. The second section shows the marking *Presto*; mm. 16–23

If the performance marking *Presto* does nothing but describe the musical effect, the tempo is 48 BPM.[49] If the marking *Presto* were to increase the number of shortest notes per tactus, the tempo would be 72 BPM.[50] Later in his life, Bach was known to be acquainted with the Silesian lutenists Sylvius Leopold Weiss and Johann Kropfgans, both famous virtuosos.[51] However, at 48 BPM the independent voices are easily distinguishable, while at 72 BPM they are difficult to discern. This suggests that the *Presto* marking (which is shown in only one of the three surviving eighteenth-century manuscripts) does not increase the number of shortest notes per tactus, and that the tempo is 48 BPM.

The first section of the KP2 sinfonia (ex. 7.14A) uses the thirty-second as shortest note and shows the performance marking *Grave. Adagio*. Because the marking *Grave. Adagio* decreases the number of shortest notes per tactus, the tempo is 36 BPM.[52] The second section, marked *Andante* (ex. 7.14B), continues to use the time signature **C**. Although there

---

47 Library Catalog Number: II 4093.
48 NBA *Kritischer Bericht*, V/10, 118.
49 4 sixteenth notes per tactus x 72 BPM ÷ 6 sixteenth notes per dotted quarter note.
50 6 replaces 4 as the number of sixteenth notes per tactus.
51 David and Mendel, *New Bach Reader*, 204. In a 1739 letter to Cantor Johann Wilhelm Koch, Bach's private secretary (and second cousin) Johann Elias Bach writes, "something extra fine in the way of music was going on, my honored cousin [second cousin, once removed] from Dresden [Wilhelm Friedemann Bach], who was here for over four weeks, having made himself heard several times at our house along with the two famous lutenists Mr. Weise [sic] and Mr. Kropffgans [sic]."
52 4 (rather than 6) thirty-second notes per tactus x 72 BPM ÷ 8 thirty-second notes per quarter note.

20 ∞ THE DANCE SUITES

is one sixty-fourth note in measure 29 (ex. 7.14C), it is clearly ornamental, so the shortest note in this section is also the thirty-second. The marking *Andante* decreases the number of shortest notes per tactus, so the tempo remains 36 BPM to the quarter note (or 72 BPM to the eighth note). In the third section, the time signature changes to $\frac{3}{4}$ (ex. 7.14C), the shortest note is now the sixteenth, and there is no performance marking. The tempo is 72 BPM,[53] twice as fast as the tempo of the first two sections. "In operas and other extended vocal works of the 17th and 18th centuries, [a sinfonia is] an instrumental piece serving as a prelude or overture."[54] Perhaps Bach titled this movement Sinfonia instead of Overture because it has three sections rather than a French overture's customary two. More speculatively, perhaps Bach has here combined elements of French and Italian overtures, with the first and third sections having features of a French overture and the second and third sections having features of an Italian overture.

EXAMPLE 7.14 Sinfonia from *Keyboard Partita 2* (BWV 826/1)

A. The beginning of the first section, which is marked *Grave Adagio*

B. The beginning of the second section, which begins in measure 8 and is marked *Andante*; mm. 7–9

C. The end of the second section and the beginning of the third; the third section begins in measure 30 and lacks a performance marking; mm. 29–32

---

53 4 sixteenth notes per tactus x 72 BPM ÷ 4 sixteenth notes per quarter note.
54 Randel, ed., *The Harvard Dictionary*, 781.

Summary

- Seventeen introductory movements, including the six *English Suite* preludes, are single-section movements. Their tempos are shown in table 7.3.

TABLE 7.3 Bach's single-section introductory movements, grouped by meter type and by tempo

Meter Type	Compound			Simple			
Tempo	48 BPM	54 BPM	72 BPM	54 BPM	61 BPM	72 BPM	81 BPM
	ES3, ES5	KP3, CS6	ES1, ES6	KP1	KP6	ES2, KP5, VP3, CS1, CS3	ES4, LS2, CS2, CS4

- Five introductory movements have two or three sections. They all exhibit features of the French overture, with a slow first section with dotted rhythms, and with a livelier, imitative, final section. Their tempos are shown in table 7.4.

TABLE 7.4 Bach's multi-section introductory movements, grouped by first section tempo, and by second section tempo

First Section Tempo	Second Section Tempo		
	48 BPM	54 BPM	72 BPM
36 BPM			KP2*
54 BPM	LS1		
61 BPM		KP4, FO, CS5	

* Note: The first and second sections of KP2 have the tempo 36 BPM. The third section has the tempo 72 BPM.

Further Thought

In modern performance practice, a prelude is often considered to be a virtuosic movement. Given the prelude's original purpose (improvisation used by the performer to warm up, check tuning, establish tonality, and attract attention), one should expect something more relaxed. Bach's proportional method yields moderate tempos for these preludes in accord with that expectation (ranging from 36 BPM to 81 BPM), rather than the virtuosic tempos often heard today.

8
Allemandes and Allemandas

The allemande (sometimes spelled allemanda, almain, almayn, or alman) originated in the sixteenth century. *Allemande* is the French word for "German."

Historical References to the Dancing of the Allemande

Thoinot Arbeau (1519–1595),[1] a French cleric and author, writing in his dance manual *Orchésographie* in 1588, describes this dance,

> The Alman is a simple rather sedate dance, familiar to the Germans, and, I believe, one of our oldest since we are descended from them. You can dance it in company, because when you have joined hands with a damsel several others may fall in line behind you, each with his partner. And you will all dance together in duple time, moving forwards, or if you wish backwards, three steps and one *grève* [raise one leg in front], or *pied en l'air* [kick one foot in the air] without *saut* [jump]; and in certain parts by one step and one *grève* or *pied en l'air*. When you have reached the end of the hall you can dance while turning around without letting go of your damsel, and the dancers who follow you will do the same. When the musicians finish this part each dancer stops and engages in light converse with his damsel and then you will begin all over again for the second part. When you come to the third part you will dance it to a quicker, more lively duple time with the same steps but introducing little springs as in the coranto. You will grasp this easily by the tabulation, which is scarcely necessary in view of the fact that there are no variations in the movements. However, in order that the whole may be perfectly clear, I shall not spare myself the pains of giving it to you in writing.
>
> Note that in the last two bars there is only one step and one *grève* in each, because the melody requires this. The minims omitted here are replaced by rests and pauses, or the little springs, that, as has been said, are used in the coranto. In dancing the Alman the young men sometimes steal the damsels from their partners and he who has been robbed seeks to obtain another damsel. But I do not hold with this behaviour because it may lead to quarrels and heart burning.[2]

Historical References to the Music for the Allemande

The allemande was often performed instrumentally even when not danced. As we saw in the introduction (page 4), it became one of the four core movements of the dance suite. Originally, the allemande formed the first movement of the suite. Later, it was almost always preceded by an introductory movement, often called a prelude.[3]

---

1 Thoinot Arbeau is the anagrammatic pen name of French cleric Jehan Tabourot.
2 Arbeau, *Orchésographie*, 125.
3 Randel, ed., *The Harvard Dictionary*, 34.

In early English sources, the allemande is described as a fast dance:
- The English composer Thomas Mace (1613–1709) writes in London in 1676, "Allmaines are Lessons very Ayrey, and Lively; and Generally of Two Strains, of the Common or Plaine-Time."[4]

Later, in France and Germany, the allemande was usually slower and more serious:
- Bach's cousin Johann Gottfried Walther (1684–1748), a Thuringian music theorist, organist, composer, and lexicographer, writes in Berlin in 1732 that an allemande serves "in a musical suite like the introduction . . . it is a serious and stately tune and should be rendered in such manner."[5]
- Johann Mattheson (1681–1764), a Hamburg composer, writer, lexicographer, diplomat, and music theorist, writes in Hamburg in 1739,

> The Allemande, as a true German invention, precedes the courante, as the latter goes before the sarabande and gigue, the sequence of which we call a Suite. Now the allemande is an arpeggiated, serious and well-composed harmony, expressing satisfaction or amusement, and delighting in order and calm.[6]

Daniel Gottlob Türk (1750–1813), a Saxon composer, organist, and music professor, writing in 1789 in Halle, Germany, presents two conflicting descriptions of tempo:

> The allemande is in 4-4 measure, begins with an upbeat, is performed in a serious manner, and is not played too fast. It occurs often in suites and partitas. The designation supposedly comes from the Allemanen, an old German people (the Swabians).
>
> A second type is also used as a dance composition. This type is in 2-4 measure and has a lively character; therefore it requires a light execution as well as a rapid tempo.[7]

Bach's Allemandes

Table 8.1 (following page) gives the number of allemandes and doubles in each set of suites. The time signature for all these movements is either **C** or **₵**. While most of them have no notes shorter than thirty-seconds, KP6, VP1, and CS6 also include sixty-fourth notes. We shall examine these three movements, as well as the double in VP1, only after we examine Bach's more typical allemandes. Interestingly, two of these movements, KP6 and VP1, are titled Allemanda, rather than Allemande.

Bach's typical allemandes (that is, the twenty-four allemandes lacking sixty-fourth notes) all include sixteenth notes, while eighteen also include at least some thirty-second notes. Table 8.2 groups them by time signature and by the percent of beats that include thirty-second notes. Where the shortest note is the thirty-second, Bach's tempo for a movement in **C** (and thus using the normal tactus) is 54 BPM,[8] while his tempo for a movement

---

4 Mace, *Musick's Monument*, 129.
5 Walther, *Musikalisches Lexikon*, 31.
6 Mattheson, *Der Volkommene Capellmeister*, 343.
7 Türk, *School of Clavier Playing*, 393.
8 6 thirty-second notes per tactus x 72 BPM ÷ 8 thirty-second notes per quarter note.

in ₵ (and thus using the accelerated tactus) is 61 BPM.⁹ Six movements, surrounded by a box in table 8.2 (FS3, FS4, KP1, LS1, CS1, and CS4), do not have any thirty-second notes at all and thus have the sixteenth as shortest note.

TABLE 8.1 The seven sets of suites in our study and the number of allemandes, allemandas, and doubles in each set

Name of Work	Number of Allemandes	Number of Allemandas	Number of Doubles	Suites That Lack Allemandes
English Suites	6			
French Suites	6			
Keyboard Partitas	5	1		
French Overture				FO
Lute Suites	1			LS2
Violin Partitas	1	1	1	VP3
Cello Suites	6			
Totals	25	2	1	

TABLE 8.2 Bach's typical allemandes, grouped by time signature, and by the percent of beats that include thirty-second notes

Percent of Beats With Thirty-Second Notes	Time Signature	
	c	₵
65% or greater	FS2, KP3, CS3	
25% to 65%	KP4*	
10% to 25%	ES4,* ES6, KP5,* VP2	KP2
1% to 10%	ES1, ES2, ES3, ES5, FS1, FS5, FS6, CS2	CS5
0%	FS3, FS4, KP1, LS1	CS1, CS4

Note 1: A box surrounds the six allemandes whose tempo departs from the rules of the proportional method, as described in the text.

Note 2: This table excludes the allemandes from *Keyboard Partita 6*, *Violin Partita 1*, and *Cello Suite 6* because they include sixty-fourth notes.

*These three allemandes contain sixteenth note triplets as well as sixteenth notes and thirty-second notes.

---

9   81 BPM replaces 72 BPM as the tactus speed.

Where the shortest note is the sixteenth, Bach's tempo for a movement using **C** is 72 BPM,[10] while his tempo for a movement using ₵ is 81 BPM.[11] Did Bach intend that some normal-tactus allemandes be played at 54 BPM and some at 72 BPM even though he gave them identical titles and time signatures? Similarly, did he intend that some accelerated-tactus allemandes be played at 61 BPM and some at 81 BPM even though he gave them identical titles and time signatures?

Thesis of This Chapter

We propose the following answer to the above questions:

- The tempo is 54 BPM for all allemandes that use **C** and 61 BPM for all allemandes that use ₵, even for those lacking thirty-second notes.

Presentation of the Material

We divide each chapter's conclusions into a series of statements called "propositions." In the text following each proposition, we present the logic that supports that proposition.

PROPOSITION 1: The tempo of the *English Suite* allemandes assumes the presence of essential thirty-second notes.

The six *English Suite* allemandes (ex. 8.1) all use the time signature **C** and include thirty-second notes in addition to sixteenth notes. The many thirty-seconds in ES4 and ES6 are clearly essential. The remaining four ES preludes each have two or more seemingly ornamental thirty-second notes (thirty-seconds appear later in the movement in ES1, ES2, and ES3). As usual, 54 BPM is the tempo for a normal-tactus movement where the beat note is the quarter and the shortest note is the thirty-second. At 54 BPM all six of these movements establish a serious, deliberate, stately motion, consistent with contemporaneous descriptions. Even the four movements with very few thirty-second notes are musically convincing at 54 BPM. Because they all use **C** (and thus use the same tactus), and they all have the same title, we conclude that they all have the same tempo. Therefore, the tempo for *English Suite* allemandes is 54 BPM even when they do not contain essential thirty-second notes.

EXAMPLE 8.1 The *English Suite* allemandes all use the time signature **C** and have the thirty-second note as shortest note

A. Allemande from *English Suite 1* (BWV 806/2); mm. 1–2

---

10 4 sixteenth notes per tactus x 72 BPM ÷ 4 sixteenth notes per quarter note.
11 81 BPM replaces 72 BPM as the tactus speed.

26 ∞ THE DANCE SUITES

EXAMPLE **8.1, cont.**

B. Allemande from *English Suite 2* (BWV 807/2); mm. 1–3

C. Allemande from *English Suite 3* (BWV 808/2); mm. 1–3

D. Allemande from *English Suite 4* (BWV 809/2); mm. 1–2

E. Allemande from *English Suite 5* (BWV 810/2); mm. 1–2

F. Allemande from *English Suite 6* (BWV 811/2); mm. 1–3

PROPOSITION 2: The tempos of later-composed allemandes assume the presence of thirty-second notes.

All fourteen remaining allemandes in ¢ include sixteenth notes (ex. 8.2), as with the *English Suites* allemandes.[12] Ten also include thirty-second notes, ranging in number from only one in FS6 to very many in KP3. The tempo is 54 BPM[13] for all fourteen movements, even for the four (FS3, FS4, KP1, and LS1) that lack thirty-second notes. This tempo gives them a serious and stately musical effect in accord with contemporaneous descriptions.

EXAMPLE 8.2 The fourteen allemandes (in addition to the *English Suite* allemandes) that use the time signature ¢

A. Allemande from *French Suite 1* (BWV 812/1); mm. 1–3

B. Allemande from *French Suite 2* (BWV 813/1); mm. 1–2

C. Allemande from *French Suite 3* (BWV 814/1); mm. 1–3

D. Allemande from *French Suite 4* (BWV 815/1); mm. 1–2

---

12 Thirty-second notes appear later in FS1, FS6, VP2, CS2, and CS3.
13 6 thirty-second notes per tactus x 72 BPM ÷ 8 thirty-second notes per quarter note.

EXAMPLE 8.2, cont.

E. Allemande from *French Suite 5* (BWV 816/1); mm. 1–3

F. Allemande from *French Suite 6* (BWV 817/1); mm. 1–3

G. Allemande from *Keyboard Partita 1* (BWV 825/2); mm. 1–3

H. Allemande from *Keyboard Partita 3* (BWV 827/2); m. 1

I. Allemande from *Keyboard Partita 4* (BWV 828/2); mm. 1–3

EXAMPLE 8.2, cont.

J. Allemande from *Keyboard Partita 5* (BWV 829/2); mm. 1–2

K. Allemande from *Lute Suite 1* (BWV 996/2); mm. 1–2

L. Allemande from *Violin Partita 2* (BWV 1004/1); mm. 1–2

M. Allemande from *Cello Suite 2* (BWV 1008/2); mm. 1–2

N. Allemande from *Cello Suite 3* (BWV 1009/2); mm. 1–3

Sources disagree on the time signatures for the CS1, CS4, and CS5 allemandes. A manuscript in the handwriting of Bach's wife Anna Magdalena Bach and the NBA both show ₵ for all three movements (ex. 8.3, following page). The BG shows C. Because the Magdalena Bach manuscript and recent scholarship agree, and because it seems more likely that a copyist or editor might omit a stroke rather than add one, we conclude that ₵ is the signature for these movements. ₵ is also the signature for the KP2 allemande (ex. 8.3D). These movements thus all use the accelerated tactus. As in the *English Suite* allemandes, the thirty-second note is assumed to be the shortest note value, even in the two (CS1 and CS4) where there are no thirty-seconds. Because of the accelerated tactus, their tempo is 61 BPM,[14] one-eighth faster than the allemandes in C, yielding musical effects consistent with contemporaneous descriptions.

---

14 81 BPM replaces 72 BPM as the tactus speed.

30 ∞ THE DANCE SUITES

EXAMPLE 8.3 Four later-composed allemandes use the time signature ¢

A. Allemande from *Cello Suite 1* (BWV 1007/2); mm. 1–2

B. Allemande from *Cello Suite 4* (BWV 1010/2); mm. 1–3

C. Allemande from *Cello Suite 5* (BWV 1011/2); this movement uses a non-standard scordatura; mm. 1–4

D. Allemande from *Keyboard Partita 2* (BWV 826/2); mm. 1–2

Note: These scans from the *Bach Gesellschaft* of the allemandes from *Cello Suite 1*, *Cellos Suite 4*, and *Cello Suite 5* have been adjusted to show the signature ¢ for reasons presented in the text.

> PROPOSITION 3: The tempos of the KP6 and VP1 allemandas and the VP1 allemanda double follow the rules of the proportional method exactly.

Bach uses the title Allemanda, rather than Allemande, in the published edition of KP6 (ex. 8.4A) and in the autograph score of VP1 (ex. 8.4B). He also includes sixty-fourth notes in both (sixty-fourth notes appear later in KP6). Should these two allemandas have the same tempo as the allemandes where the time signature is ¢ and where the shortest note is either the sixteenth or the thirty-second (54 BPM)? These two movements do not sound serious and stately at 54 BPM. Further, the VP1 allemanda in particular would be challenging to perform at 54 BPM. It seems likely that Bach intended that these two movements be played at the tempo implied by the presence of sixty-fourth notes (36 BPM)[15] rather than at the tempo of Bach's more typical allemandes (54 BPM).

These two movements share a characteristic rhythmic figure (circled in ex. 8.5). This figure does not appear in any other titled Bach allemande.[16] Thus, this figure, the presence of sixty-fourth notes, and the unusual title Allemanda, could be Bach's "signposts" that these two movements are similar to each other but different from the typical allemande.

---

15 8 sixty-fourth notes per tactus x 72 BPM ÷ 16 sixty-fourth notes per quarter note.

16 This figure does, however, appear in at least one other work, "Komm, süßes Kreuz" from the *St. Matthew Passion* (BWV 244/57).

EXAMPLE 8.4 Two allemandas include sixty-fourth notes

A. Allemanda from *Keyboard Partita 6* (BWV 830/2); mm. 1–2 (sixty-fourth notes appear later)

B. Allemanda from *Violin Partita 1* (BWV 1002/1); mm. 1–3a

EXAMPLE 8.5 The allemanda's characteristic rhythmic figure, enclosed by ovals

A. Allemanda from *Keyboard Partita 6* (BWV 830/2); mm. 13–14

B. Allemanda from *Violin Partita 1* (BWV 1002/1); mm. 17–18

In the autograph score Bach uses the title Allemanda for VP2 (see ex. 8.2L, page 29). We discussed this movement on page 27 where we concluded that the tempo for all of Bach's normal-tactus allemandes that lack sixty-fourth notes should be 54 BPM. Should we reconsider this conclusion? Could the title Allemanda used in VP2 indicate that this movement, too, uses the tempo 36 BPM? Probably not. Bach was not always consistent in his use of titles for his dance movements (see for example the discussion of courantes and correntes on page 37). Further, the other two signposts (sixty-fourth notes and the above characteristic rhythmic figure) are not present. More importantly, this movement would be unmusically slow at 36 BPM.

32 ∞ THE DANCE SUITES

The double (ex. 8.6) that follows the VP1 allemanda has the quarter as beat note and the sixteenth as shortest note. Because the autograph score[17] and the NBA both show the signature ¢ for this movement, we reject the signature C shown in the BG. Thus, the tactus is accelerated and the tempo is 81 BPM,[18] more than twice as fast as the tempo of the allemanda itself (36 BPM). In VP1, Bach clearly explored the use of doubles. Of Bach's thirty suites, only six include doubles, one double each in ES2, ES3, ES6, and LS2, two in ES1, but **four** in VP1. Of special note is that the only doubles with a different tempo from that of the related dance are in VP1 (the allemanda and the sarabande). Also unique is Bach's only use of an Italian performance marking in a double (VP1 corrente double).

EXAMPLE 8.6 Allemanda Double from *Violin Partita 1* (BWV 1002/2); mm. 1–3

Note: While the *Bach Gesellschaft* shows the signature C for this movement, the above scan of the *Bach Gesellschaft* has been adjusted to show the signature ¢ for reasons presented in the text.

> PROPOSITION 4: The tempo for the CS6 allemande is 54 BPM; it has the eighth note as beat note.

The CS6 allemande (ex. 8.7A) is a special case because it has the one-hundred-twenty-eighth note as shortest note (one-hundred-twenty-eighth notes appear later). Considering the eighth as beat note, the proportional tempo would be 54 BPM.[19] This tempo is musically convincing, and it is the same as the tempo of the *English Suite* allemandes.

EXAMPLE 8.7 The notation of Allemande from *Cello Suite 6* (BWV 1012/2) is unusually complicated

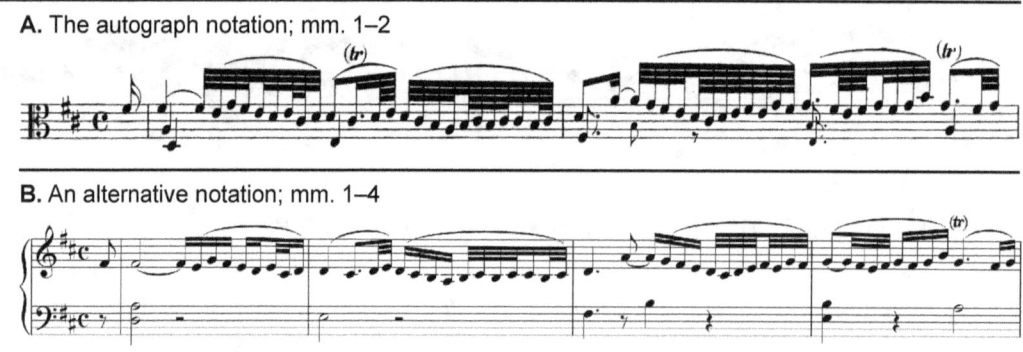

A. The autograph notation; mm. 1–2

B. An alternative notation; mm. 1–4

Note: This allemande also uses scordatura.

---

17 Library Catalog Number: P 967.
18 4 sixteenth notes per tactus x 81 BPM ÷ 4 sixteenth notes per quarter note.
19 12 one-hundred-twenty-eighth notes per tactus x 72 BPM ÷ 16 one-hundred-twenty-eighth notes per eighth note.

In ex. 8.7B (preceding page), we re-notate the first two measures of ex. 8.7A with the quarter as beat note rather than the eighth.[20] Each measure of the original is expanded into two measures in this alternative notation. Considering the resulting sixty-fourth notes as ornamental, the thirty-second note is the shortest essential note value. The proportional tempo, now with the quarter note beat, remains 54 BPM.

Clearly Bach's autograph notation in this allemande is much more difficult to read than that of Bach's other allemandes. Why did Bach make it more difficult to read? Was he trying to challenge a particular hotshot performer?

Summary

The tempos for Bach's allemandes are listed in table 8.3.

- The majority are titled Allemande and include no notes shorter than the thirty-second. The tempo is 54 BPM for the twenty-one movements using the signature C (and therefore the normal tactus) and 61 BPM for the four movements using the signature ₵ (and therefore the accelerated tactus).
- VP1 and KP6 are titled Allemanda and include sixty-fourth notes in addition to thirty-second notes. Their tempo is 36 BPM.

Bach's notation of the CS6 allemande is unusual because it uses the one-hundred-twenty-eighth note as shortest note. When re-notated using note values that are twice as long, the movement is revealed to be a typical C allemande.

TABLE 8.3 Bach's allemandes and allemandas, grouped by tempo and by percentage of beats including thirty-second notes

Percentage of Beats Including Thirty-Second Notes	Tempo		
	36 BPM (Allemanda)	54 BPM (Allemande)	61 BPM (Allemande)
65% or greater	VP1, KP6	FS2, KP3, CS3	
25% to 65%		KP4	
10% to 25%		ES4, ES6, KP5, VP2, CS6*	KP2
1% to 10%		ES1, ES2, ES3, ES5, FS1, FS5, FS6, CS2	CS5
0%		FS3, FS4, KP1, LS1	CS1, CS4

* In this table, the *Cello Suite 6* allemande is grouped based on the alternative notation presented on the preceding page.

---

20 On the third quarter note in measure 2 of the original Bach uses a variable dot, a common eighteenth-century shorthand. In ex. 8.7B the variable dot is replaced with a tie.

9
Courantes and Correntes

The courante and the corrente originated in the sixteenth century. *Courante* (French) and *corrente* (Italian) are derived from the Latin word *currere*, which means "to run."

Historical References to the Dancing of the Courante

- The French cleric and author Thoinot Arbeau (1519–1595),[1] writing in his dance manual *Orchésographie* in 1588, states that the coranto is danced in a "light duple time." Other writers refer to both the courante and the corrente as triple-meter dances. Arbeau further states that "the steps of the coranto must be executed with a spring." He continues,

  > In my youth there was a kind of game or mime arranged to the coranto. Three young men would choose three young girls, and, having ranged themselves in a row, the first dancer would lead his damsel to the other end of the room and then return alone to his companions. The second dancer would do the same, then the third, so that the three girls were left segregated at one end of the room and the three young men at the other. And when the third dancer had returned, the first one, playing the fool and making amorous grimaces and gestures while pulling up his hose and adjusting his shirt, went off to claim his damsel who refused his suit and turned her back upon him, until, seeing the young man was returning to his place, she feigned despair. The other two did the same. Finally they all three advanced together, each to claim his own damsel and to implore her favour upon bended knee with clasped hands. Whereupon the damsels fell into their arms and they all danced the coranto helter-skelter.[2]

- Michael Praetorius (1571–1621), a Thuringian composer and music theorist, writes in 1619 that courantes involve "certain measured up and down skips, similar to running while dancing."[3]
- In seventeenth-century Italy the corrente was a cheerful courtship dance.[4] It is often described using the word *running*. For example, the English lexicographer James Grassineau (c. 1715–?) writes in 1740 that the corrente is "a sort of quick running *French* dance."[5]

---

1 As mentioned in footnote 1 on page 22, Thoinot Arbeau is the anagrammatic pen name of French cleric Jehan Tabourot.
2 Arbeau, *Orchésographie*, 123.
3 Praetorius, *Syntagma Musicum III*, 42.
4 Randell, ed., *The Harvard Dictionary*, 221–22.
5 Grassineau, ed. and trans., *A Musical Dictionary*, 46.

- Other writers refer to a slower pace. In 1717 Gottfried Taubert (1679–1746), a Thuringian dance master who worked in Leipzig for a portion of the time Bach lived there, published an encyclopedic treatise covering the world of dance. In it, Taubert includes three choreographies of the courante. The American music and dance historians Little and Jenne interpret the notation of the simplest of these three choreographies:

  > The gentleman holds the lady's left hand throughout the dance. They begin at the foot of the hall, move up the hall, turn widely leftward, and come back, forming an oval or an ellipse. The lady moves on the outside of the turns with larger steps, the gentleman inside.[6]

- Pierre Rameau (1674–1748), the dancing master to Elisabetta Farnese (Queen of Spain from 1714 to 1746), writes about the courante in 1725 in Paris:

  > Formerly, the *Courante* was much in fashion, and as it is a very solemn dance with a nobler style and grander manners than the others, is very varied in its figures, and has dignified and distinguished movements, Louis XIV, of happy memory, was pleased to prefer it.
  >
  > For after the *Branles* with which, as I have already stated, all Court Balls were and are still begun, His Majesty danced the Courante. Indeed, he danced it better than any member of his Court and with a quite unusual grace.
  >
  > But what testifies still more to the attachment and preference he had for the dance is that, despite the weighty affairs which continually occupied the mighty conqueror, he never failed to set aside some hours each day for the practice of it, throughout all the twenty-two years that Monsieur Beauchamps had the honour to instruct him in this noble exercise.[7]

Historical References to the Music for the Courante

As with other Baroque court dances, the music that was used to accompany the courante dance became popular for its own sake. In most sources the courante is described as grave and serious:

- Bach's cousin Johann Gottfried Walther (1684–1748), a Thuringian music theorist, organist, and composer, writes in 1732, "The tune of the Courante, or rather the rhythm of the Courante dance, is absolutely the most serious one can find."[8]
- Johann Joachim Quantz (1697–1773), a composer and flutist, writes in 1752, "The *entrée*, the *loure*, and the *courante* are played majestically, and the bow is detached at each crochet [quarter note], whether it is dotted or not."[9]
- Daniel Gottlob Türk (1750–1813), a Saxon composer, organist, and music professor, writes in 1789, "The *courante (corrente)* is in $\frac{3}{2}$ (or $\frac{3}{4}$) measure and commonly begins with a short note as upbeat. It was—at least formerly—used as a dance and

---

6 Little and Jenne, *Dance and the Music of J. S. Bach*, 116.
7 Rameau, *The Dancing Master*, 74–75.
8 Walther, *Musikalisches Lexicon*, 175.
9 Quantz, *The Art of Playing the Flute*, 291.

consisted of a combination of many running figures. Its execution must be serious, but almost more detached than legato. The tempo is not very fast."[10]

Other writers seem to refer to the courante as a faster movement.

- Thomas Mace (c. 1613–1709), an English composer, writing in London in 1676 states, "*Corantoes*, are *Lessons* of a *Shorter Cut*, and of a *Quicker Triple-Time*; commonly of 2 *Strains*, and full of *Sprightfulness*, and *Vigour, Lively, Brisk*, and *Cheerful*."[11] However, while Mace refers to the courante as "quicker," just before that he describes the galliard as grave and sober. Mace may be indicating merely that the courante is quicker than the grave and sober galliard.
- Georg Muffat (1653–1704), an Alsacian composer and organist, published a set of dance pieces in 1698. In the introduction to this work, he included instructions on bowing the violin in the style of Lully. Originally published in four languages (Latin, French, German, and Italian), these instructions include a brief discussion of the courante, including a musical example. Here, Muffat states that odd-numbered measures should begin with a down bow, while even-numbered measures should begin with an up bow. In his 2001 English translation, David K. Wilson gives as the reason, "because of the fast tempo."[12] However, in the French text, Muffat gives as the reason, "because of the speed of the movement of the notes."[13] Similarly, in the German text, Muffat gives as the reason, "because of the exceptional vigor of the notes."[14] Thus, Muffat may be indicating not that the tempo is fast, but rather that the number of divisions of the beat results in fast notes.[15]
- Johann Mattheson (1681–1764), a Hamburg composer, writer, diplomat, and music theorist, writing in Leipzig in 1739, stresses the use of the courante as a showpiece: "The lutenists' masterpiece, especially in France, is usually the courante, to which one applies his toil and art to advantage." Here, the word *masterpiece* may refer to rhythmic and contrapuntal complexity and increased use of ornamentation. Mattheson does not speak of tempo. Instead, he refers to the courante as "chiefly characterized by the passion or mood of sweet expectation. For there is something heartfelt, something longing and also gratifying, in this melody: clearly music on which hopes are built."[16]

---

10 Türk, *School of Clavier Playing*, 394.
11 Mace, *Musick's Monument*, 129.
12 Wilson, ed., *Georg Muffat on Performance Practice*, 39.
13 Muffat, *Florilegium Secundum*, 46; "pour la vitesse du mouvement les notes."
14 Muffat, *Florilegium Secundum*, 22; "eylendshalber außgenohmen die Noten."
15 Little and Jenne, *Dance and the Music of J. S. Bach*, 115.
16 Mattheson, *Der vollkommene Capellmeister*, 342; "Der Lautenisten Meisterstück, absonderlich in Frankreich, ist gemeiniglich die Courante, worauf man auch seine Mühe und Kunst nicht übel anwendet. Die Leidenschafft oder Gemüths-Bewegung, welche in einer Courante vorgetragen werden soll, ist die süsse Hoffnung. Denn es findet sich was hertzhafftes, was verlangendes und auch was erfreuliches in dieser Melodie: lauter Stücke, daraus die Hoffnung zusammengefüget wird."

Musicians today recognize two main styles of this dance, French-style courantes with frequent syncopations, dotted rhythms, and a texture of three or more voices, and Italian-style correntes with consistent motion of the shortest note value and a texture of only two voices.

Bach's Courantes and Correntes

Table 9.1 gives the number of courantes, correntes, and courante doubles in each set of suites (ES1 contains two courantes). In his early works, Bach used the title Courante for those in the Italian style as well as for those in the French style. Beginning with his publication of *Keyboard Partita 1* in 1726, Bach adopted what has become standard practice by using the title Corrente for those in the Italian style. We categorize those in the French style as "courantes" and those in the Italian style as "correntes," regardless of Bach's titles. The suites in our study contain fourteen French-style courantes and fifteen Italian-style correntes.

TABLE 9.1 The seven sets of suites in our study and the number of courantes, correntes, and doubles in each set

Name of Work	Number of Courantes	Number of Correntes	Number of Doubles	Suites That Lack Courantes or Correntes
English Suites	7		2	
French Suites	2	4		
Keyboard Partitas	2	4		
French Overture	1			
Lute Suites	1			LS2
Violin Partitas		2		VP3
Cello Suites	1	5		
Totals	14	15	2	

Thesis of This Chapter

The tempos of Bach's courantes and correntes follow the rules of the proportional method exactly, except that sixteenth notes and thirty-second notes in courantes (but not in correntes) are always considered ornamental.

PROPOSITION 1: The tempo of the *English Suite* courantes assumes that sixteenth notes (and thirty-second notes) are ornamental.

Table 9.2 groups Bach's French-style courantes by time signature, tactus speed, and shortest note. For ES1, where there are two courantes, we show Courante I as ES1(C1) and Courante II as ES1(C2).

TABLE 9.2 Bach's courantes, grouped by time signature, tactus speed, and shortest note value

Time Signature	Tactus Speed	Shortest Note Value		
		♪	♬	♬
3/2	normal	ES1(C1)	ES1(C2), ES2, ES3, ES4, ES6, FS1, KP4	ES5, LS1
3/2	accelerated		KP2, FO, CS5	
6/4	normal		FS3	

All seven prototypical *English Suite* courantes (ex. 9.1, following page) use the time signature 3/2, the half as beat note, and the normal tactus. For ES1 Courante I, the shortest note value is the eighth. All others also include sixteenth notes and one even has thirty-second notes (ES5), but all these shorter values seem ornamental. If the sixteenth notes were considered essential, the resulting tempo would be 36 BPM,[17] which would be much too slow. If the thirty-second notes were considered essential, the tempo would be an impossibly slow 27 BPM.[18] If both the sixteenth notes and the thirty-second notes are considered ornamental, the tempo is an appropriate and majestic 54 BPM.[19] Thus, the sixteenth and thirty-second notes in these courantes must be considered ornamental, and the tempo is 54 BPM.

Some may suggest that these courantes should be played faster than the proportional tempo of 54 BPM. To increase the tempo, one might increase the number of shortest notes per tactus from three to four, thereby increasing the tempo to 72 BPM.[20] However, at 54 BPM all seven have a solemn and serious musical effect, consistent with contemporaneous descriptions. At 72 BPM they do not.

---

17 4 sixteenth notes per tactus x 72 BPM ÷ 8 sixteenth notes per half note.
18 6 thirty-second notes per tactus x 72 BPM ÷ 16 thirty-second notes per half note.
19 3 eighth notes per tactus x 72 BPM ÷ 4 eighth notes per half note.
20 4 replaces 3 as the number of eighth notes per tactus.

Courantes and Correntes ∞ 39

EXAMPLE 9.1 The courantes from the *English Suites* all use the time signature $\frac{3}{2}$ and the normal tactus

A. Courante I from *English Suite 1* (BWV 806/3); mm. 1–3

B. Courante II from *English Suite 1* (BWV 806/4); mm. 1–3

C. Courante from *English Suite 2* (BWV 807/3); mm. 1–3

D. Courante from *English Suite 3* (BWV 808/3); mm. 1–4

E. Courante from *English Suite 4* (BWV 809/3); mm. 1–3

F. Courante from *English Suite 5* (BWV 810/3); mm. 1–3

EXAMPLE 9.1, cont.

G. Courante from *English Suite 6* (BWV 811/3); mm. 1–3

Bach includes two doubles following the second courante from ES1 (ex. 9.2). Because they share the features of the courante that precedes them (sixteenths appear later in the second double), they have the same tempo (54 BPM).

EXAMPLE 9.2 The two doubles in *English Suite 1*

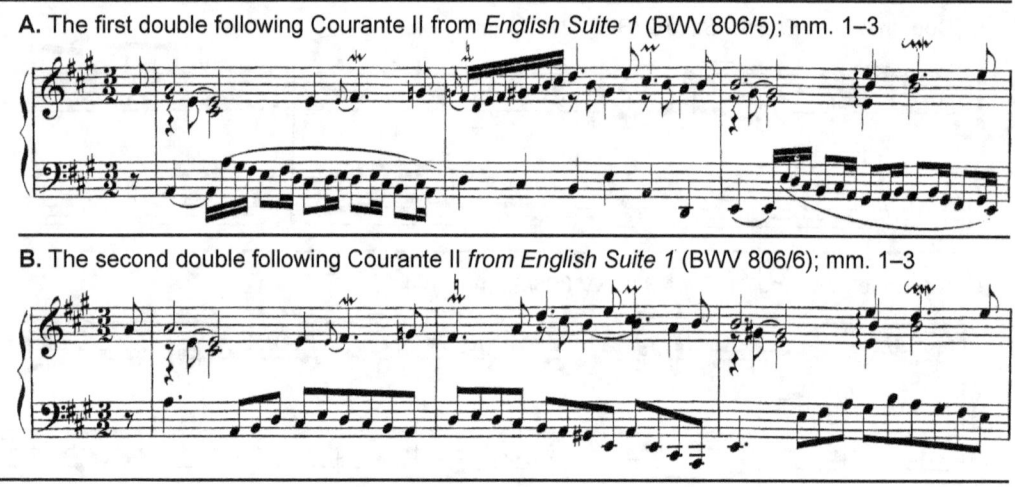

A. The first double following Courante II from *English Suite 1* (BWV 806/5); mm. 1–3

B. The second double following Courante II from *English Suite 1* (BWV 806/6); mm. 1–3

PROPOSITION 2: The tempos of later-composed $\frac{3}{2}$ courantes assumes that sixteenth notes (and thirty-second notes) are ornamental.

Just as sixteenth notes (and thirty-second notes) in *English Suite* courantes are considered ornamental, so are those in Bach's later $\frac{3}{2}$ courantes (ex. 9.3). If the sixteenth notes in these courantes were considered essential, the tempo for the normal tactus movements (FS1, KP4, and LS1) would be 36 BPM,[21] and the tempo for the accelerated-tactus movements (KP2, FO, and CS5) would be 41 BPM.[22] Both of these tempos would be painfully slow. The title Courante tells us that the sixteenth notes are ornamental. The resulting tempos

---

21 4 sixteenth notes per tactus x 72 BPM ÷ 8 sixteenth notes per half note.
22 81 BPM replaces 72 BPM as the tactus speed.

of 54 BPM[23] (normal tactus) and 61 BPM[24] (accelerated tactus)[25] yield solemn and serious musical effects consistent with descriptions in the literature.

EXAMPLE 9.3 The six courantes (other than the *English Suite* courantes) that use the signature 3/2

A. Courante from *French Suite 1* (BWV 812/2) uses the normal tactus; mm. 1–3

B. Courante from *Keyboard Partita 2* (BWV 826/3) uses the accelerated tactus; mm. 1–3

C. Courante from *Keyboard Partita 4* (BWV 828/3) uses the normal tactus; mm. 1–3

D. Courante from *French Overture* (BWV 831/2) uses the accelerated tactus; mm. 1–3

---

23 3 eighth notes per tactus x 72 BPM ÷ 4 eighth notes per half note.
24 81 BPM replaces 72 BPM as the tactus speed.
25 The accelerated tactus was established in the preceding overture for FO and in the preceding allemandes for KP2 and CS5.

EXAMPLE 9.3, cont.

E. Courante from *Lute Suite 1* (BWV 996/3) uses the normal tactus; mm. 1–3

F. Courante from *Cello Suite 5* (BWV 1011/3) uses the accelerated tactus and scordatura; mm. 1–4

PROPOSITION 3: The tempo is 36 BPM for the FS3 courante, the only Bach courante in $\frac{6}{4}$.

This courante (ex. 9.4) uses the normal tactus, the dotted half as beat note, and the eighth as shortest essential note (the few sixteenth notes are clearly ornamental). The tempo is 36 BPM.[26] The speed of the eighth notes in this courante is the same as the speed of the eighth notes in the *English Suite* courantes (that is, three times the speed of the normal tactus).

EXAMPLE 9.4 Courante from *French Suite 3* (BWV 814/2); mm. 1–3

While the *English Suite* courantes all use the time signature $\frac{3}{2}$, both sections of all of them end in a hemiola (surrounded by a circle in ex. 9.5). The metrical sense of these hemiola measures is clearly $\frac{6}{4}$. Thus, the $\frac{6}{4}$ meter used in the FS3 courante recalls the $\frac{6}{4}$ implied by the hemiolas in the prototypical *English Suite* courantes.

EXAMPLE 9.5 The hemiola at the end of the first section of Courante I from *English Suite 1* (BWV 806/3) is here enclosed by a circle; mm. 8–11

---

26 3 eighth notes per tactus × 72 BPM ÷ 6 eighth notes per dotted half note.

PROPOSITION 4: The tempos of Bach's correntes follow the rules of the proportional method exactly.

Table 9.3 groups Bach's correntes by number of notes per beat, tactus speed, and shortest note value.

TABLE 9.3 Bach's correntes, grouped by number of notes per beat, tactus speed, and shortest note value

Number of Notes per Beat	Tactus Speed	Shortest Note Value		
		♪	♬	♬
2	normal	FS2, CS3	KP5	
	accelerated	VP1		
3	normal	FS4, KP1, VP2		
	accelerated	CS4		
4	normal		FS5, FS6, KP3, CS2, CS6	KP6
	accelerated		CS1	

Correntes Having Two Notes per Beat (four survive)

The FS2, CS3, and VP1 correntes all use the time signature ¾, the quarter as beat note, and the eighth as shortest note (ex. 9.6). FS2 and CS3 use the normal tactus, so their tempo is 108 BPM.[27] VP1 uses the accelerated tactus,[28] so its tempo is 122 BPM.[29]

EXAMPLE 9.6 The three correntes having two eighth notes per beat

A. Corrente from *French Suite 2* (BWV 813/2) uses the normal tactus; mm. 1–6

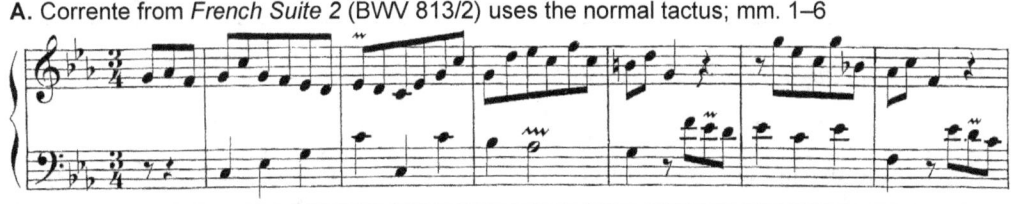

B. Corrente from *Cello Suite 3* (BWV 1009/3) uses the normal tactus; mm. 1–7

---

27 3 eighth notes per tactus x 72 BPM ÷ 2 eighth notes per quarter note.
28 The accelerated tactus is adopted from the preceding allemanda double.
29 81 BPM replaces 72 BPM as the tactus speed.

EXAMPLE 9.6, cont.

C. Corrente from *Violin Partita 1* (BWV 1002/3) uses the accelerated tactus; mm. 1–6

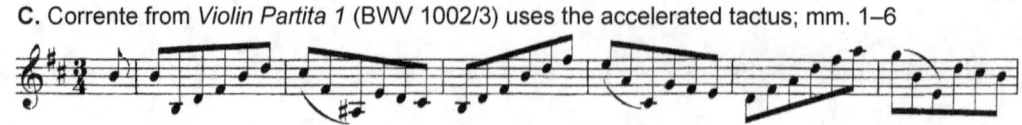

The double that follows the VP1 corrente (ex. 9.7) is a variation. The tactus, time signature, and beat note remain the same, but the shortest note is now the sixteenth. The marking *Presto* indicates that there are six sixteenth notes per tactus, rather than four, so the tempo also remains the same (122 BPM).[30] This is the only time Bach uses a performance marking in a double. (See page 32 for more information about VP1 and its doubles.)

EXAMPLE 9.7 Corrente Double from *Violin Partita 1* (BWV 1002/4); mm. 1–3

The KP5 corrente (ex. 9.8) also has two notes per beat, but here the time signature is $\frac{3}{8}$, the shortest note is the sixteenth, and the beat note in most of the movement is the eighth. Because the tactus is normal, the tempo is 144 BPM.[31] (The tempo could also be stated as 48 BPM per dotted quarter note.)

EXAMPLE 9.8 The sole corrente having two sixteenth notes per beat; Corrente from *Keyboard Partita 5* (BWV 829/3); mm. 1–6

Correntes Having Three Notes per Beat (four survive)

The FS4, KP1, VP2, and CS4 correntes all use the time signature $\frac{3}{4}$, the quarter as beat note, and the triplet eighth as shortest note (ex. 9.9). Three (FS4, KP1, and VP2) use the normal tactus, so their tempo is 72 BPM.[32] Notice the dotted-eighth-and-sixteenth figure in all three of these correntes. In appropriate performance practice, the dotted eighth note is played on the beat and the sixteenth note is played at the same time as the third note of the triplet. This is a shorthand commonly used in the eighteenth century.

---

30 6 (rather than 4) sixteenth notes per tactus x 81 BPM ÷ 4 sixteenth notes per quarter note.
31 4 sixteenth notes per tactus x 72 BPM ÷ 2 sixteenth notes per eighth note.
32 3 eighth notes per tactus x 72 BPM ÷ 3 eighth note triplets per quarter note. The tempo for these movements may also be determined assuming the sixteenth note as shortest note (4 sixteenth notes per tactus x 72 BPM ÷ 4 sixteenth notes per quarter note).

EXAMPLE 9.9 Three normal-tactus correntes have three notes per beat

A. Corrente from *French Suite 4* (BWV 815/2); mm. 1–4

B. Corrente from *Keyboard Partita 1* (BWV 825/3); mm. 1–4

C. Corrente from *Violin Partita 2* (BWV 1004/2); mm. 1–4

The features of the CS4 corrente (ex. 9.10) are the same except that the tactus is accelerated,[33] so the tempo is 81 BPM.[34] Some beats (such as the second and third beats in measure 2) contain four sixteenth notes per beat. Other beats, such as those in measure 5, contain three eighth note triplets per beat. This movement's triplets, though not constant, give it a flow in common with the other correntes with three notes per beat (FS4, KP1, and VP2).

EXAMPLE 9.10 Corrente from *Cello Suite 4* (BWV 1010/3) uses the accelerated tactus; mm. 1–5

Correntes Having Four Notes per Beat (seven survive)

The FS5, FS6, KP3, CS1, CS2, and CS6 correntes use the time signature $\frac{3}{4}$, the quarter as beat note, and the sixteenth as shortest note (ex. 9.11). All but one use the normal tactus, so their tempo is 72 BPM.[35] The exception, CS1, uses the accelerated tactus,[36] so its tempo is 81 BPM.[37]

---

33 The accelerated tactus is adopted from the preceding allemande.
34 81 BPM replaces 72 BPM as the tactus speed.
35 4 sixteenth notes per tactus x 72 BPM ÷ 4 sixteenth notes per quarter note.
36 The accelerated tactus is adopted from the preceding allemande.
37 81 BPM replaces 72 BPM as the tactus speed.

46 ∞ THE DANCE SUITES

EXAMPLE 9.11 Six correntes have four sixteenth notes per beat

The KP6 corrente (ex. 9.12) also has four notes per beat, but the time signature is $\frac{3}{8}$, the beat note is the eighth, and the shortest note is the thirty-second. Because the tactus is normal, the tempo is 108 BPM.[38]

---

38   6 thirty-second notes per tactus x 72 BPM ÷ 4 thirty-second notes per eighth note.

EXAMPLE 9.12 The sole corrente with four thirty-second notes per beat; Corrente from *Keyboard Partita 6* (BWV 830/3); mm. 1–4

Summary

French-style courantes (shown in table 9.4) include numerous syncopations and dotted rhythms, and their textures have at least three voices. They are serious and have majestic tempos:

- For those in $\frac{3}{2}$, the tempo is 54 BPM where the tactus is normal and 61 BPM where the tactus is accelerated.
- For the one courante in $\frac{6}{4}$ (FS3), the tempo is 36 BPM.
- Some courantes are highly ornamented. Ornamentation has no effect on tempo.

TABLE 9.4 The tempos of Bach's courantes

Time Signature	Tactus Speed	Tempo	Abbreviation
$\frac{6}{4}$	normal	36 BPM	FS3
$\frac{3}{2}$	normal	54 BPM	ES1(C1), ES1(C2), ES2, ES3, ES4, ES5, ES6, FS1, KP4, LS1
$\frac{3}{2}$	accelerated	61 BPM	KP2, FO, CS5

Italian-style correntes (shown in table 9.5) have tempos ranging from 72 BPM to 144 BPM. They usually exhibit consistent motion of the shortest note value and their textures have only two voices.

- Four have two notes per beat (three with eighth notes and one with sixteenth notes).
- Four have three notes per beat (eighth note triplets).
- Seven have four notes per beat (six with sixteenth notes and one with thirty-second notes).

TABLE 9.5 The tempos of Bach's correntes

Number of Notes per Beat	Tactus Speed	Number of Shortest Notes per Tactus		
		3	4	6
2	Normal	108 BPM: FS2, CS3	144 BPM: KP5	
	Accelerated	122 BPM: VP1		
3	Normal	72 BPM: FS4, KP1, VP2		
	Accelerated	81 BPM: CS4*		
4	Normal		72 BPM: FS5, FS6, KP3, CS2, CS6	108 BPM: KP6
	Accelerated		81 BPM: CS1	

*Note: Some beats of the corrente from *Cello Suite 4* have two notes per beat, some have three notes per beat, and some have four notes per beat. We group this movement with the correntes having three notes per beat because its triplets, though not constant, give it a flow in common with the other correntes with three notes per beat.

Further Thoughts

1. When played at Bach's tempos, courantes are serious and majestic, in agreement with contemporaneous descriptions. However, most of today's performances use much faster tempos. Thus, modern performance practice of the courante would appear not to be consistent with contemporaneous descriptions. It is difficult to believe that Louis XIV would have danced at tempos as frenetically fast as those chosen by a majority of recent performers. Certainly, the Sun King would have wanted his physical movements to appear dignified. Also, the position of the courante as the second dance of the Baroque suite suggests that a moderate tempo would be appropriate. The composer would save true virtuosity for the final dance in the suite.

2. After the *English Suites*, Bach composed three more six-suite sets (the *French Suites*, *Keyboard Partitas*, and *Cello Suites*). In each set he includes at least one corrente with two notes per beat, one with three notes per beat, and two with four notes per beat. Thus, it appears that Bach's correntes represent an exploration of ways to achieve variety of tempo and rhythm in music of simple-triple meter. We shall see that Bach does the same thing in music of compound meter with his gigas (see page 74).

10
Sarabandes

While the origins of the French word *sarabande*, the Italian word *sarabanda*, and the Spanish word *zarabanda* are not known with certainty, these words are clearly related.

Historical References to the Dancing of the Sarabande

- Thoinot Arbeau (1520–1595),[1] a French cleric and author (who is usually an authoritative source), makes no mention of the sarabande in his 1588 compendium of sixteenth-century court dances.[2] Miguel de Cervantes, however, in his 1615 play *The Marvellous Puppet Show*, describes the sarabande as an antique dance accompanied by castanets.[3] Because the Frenchman Arbeau seems not to have known the sarabande in 1588, while the Spaniard Cervantes describes it as antique only twenty-seven years later, the sarabande was probably introduced to French courts from Spain.

In Spain the sarabande was considered an obscene dance.[4]

- In 1603 Juan de Mariana (1536–1624), a Jesuit priest and historian, called the sarabande and its related song "so lascivious in its words and so unseemly in its motions that it is enough to inflame even very decent people."[5]
- A character in the Cervantes entre'acte *The Cave of Salamanca*, published posthumously in 1616, claims that the zarabanda's birthplace was in hell.[6]
- Battista Marino, a Neapolitan poet, writing in Paris in 1623, refers to the sarabande as an "ungodly and obscene amusement introduced from New Spain."[7] In addition to confirming the characterization of the sarabande as obscene, Marino raises the possibility that it was imported from the New World, possibly from what is now Mexico.

Kellom Tomlinson (born c. 1693), an English dance writer, presents choreography for the dance in his 1735 dancing manual. He includes musical examples for two types of sarabande, one in $\frac{3}{4}$ marked "slow" and one in $\frac{3}{2}$ marked "very slow."[8]

---

1 Thoinot Arbeau is the anagrammatic pen name of French cleric Jehan Tabourot.
2 Arbeau, *Orchésographie*.
3 Cervantes, *Entremeses*, 164. "Si es antiguo el baile de la zarabanda."
4 Stevenson, *The First Dated Mention*, 29.
5 Mariana. "Tratado contra los juegos públicos," Capitulo XII, 433.
6 Cervantes, *Entremeses*, 184. "¿Adónde? En el infierno: allí tuvieron su origen y principio."
7 Marino, *L'Adone*, canto ventesimo, 84.
8 Tomlinson, *The Art of Dancing*, book 1, plates IV and VI.

Historical References to the Music for the Sarabande

The music for the sarabande was cultivated independently from the dance itself.

- Johann Jakob Froberger (1616–1667), a Swabian composer and keyboard virtuoso, includes examples of the sarabande in his 1649 collection of dance suites.[9]
- Georg Muffat (1653–1704), an Alsacian composer and organist, writes in 1695 in the forward to his first collection of dance suites, "In $\frac{3}{2}$ the measure is quite held back, while in $\frac{3}{4}$ it is more lively, except that in Sarabands and Airs it is a bit slower."[10] Muffat probably means that $\frac{3}{4}$ sarabandes are a bit slower than other more lively $\frac{3}{4}$ movements, but not that they are slower than other $\frac{3}{2}$ movements.
- Sébastien de Brossard (1655–1730), a French theorist, defines the sarabande in his 1703 *Dictionary of Music*, "The Sarabande is essentially only a minuet whose tempo is grave, slow, serious."[11]
- James Grassineau (c. 1715–1767), an English lexicographer, published a translation and expansion of Brossard's *Dictionary* in 1740 in London. He repeats Brossard's definition, and adds, "'tis usually danced to the sound of the *Guitarre*, or *Castanettes*."[12]
- Bach's cousin Johann Gottfried Walther (1684–1748), a Thuringian theorist, organist, and composer, in 1732 writes of the sarabande, "Its stately manner is much favored and used by the Spaniards; it is generally a short tune which is beaten as a slow $\frac{3}{4}$ for dancing and $\frac{3}{2}$ for playing and has two repeats."[13]
- Frederick the Great's court musician Johann Joaquim Quantz (1697–1773), after referring to the courante as being played "majestically," writes in Dresden in 1752 that the "*sarabande* has the same movement [as the *courante*] but is played with a somewhat more agreeable execution."[14]
- Jean-Jacques Rousseau (1712–1778), the Genevan philosopher and composer, writes of the sarabande in 1768, "The air of a dance, which bears the same name, which seems to have been transmitted from Spain, and was formerly danced with castagnetto's. This dance is no longer used, unless in some old French operas. The air of the sarabande is [beaten slowly in three]."[15]
- Daniel Gottlob Türk (1750–1813), a Saxon composer, organist, and music professor, writes in Leipzig in 1792, "The *sarabande*, a dance particularly in use in Spain, is in $\frac{3}{2}$ or $\frac{3}{4}$ measure, has a serious character joined with expression and dignity, and requires therefore a rather slow tempo in addition to a heavy execution."[16]

---

9 Froberger, *Libro secondo di toccate, etc.*, 86, 89, 93, 96, 99, and 108.
10 Wilson, ed. *Georg Muffat*, 17.
11 Brossard, *Dictionary of Music*, 103.
12 Grassineau, *A Musical Dictionary*, 208.
13 Walther, *Musikalisches Lexicon*, 488.
14 Quantz, *The Art*, 291.
15 Rousseau, *A Complete Dictionary of Music*, 350.
16 Türk, *School of Clavier Playing*, 396.

Bach's Sarabandes

Table 10.1 gives the number of sarabandes and sarabande doubles in each set of suites.

TABLE 10.1 The seven sets of suites in our study and the number of sarabandes and doubles in each set

Name of Work	Number of Sarabandes	Number of Doubles	Suite That Lacks Sarabandes
English Suites	6	1	
French Suites	6		
Keyboard Partitas	6		
French Overture	1		
Lute Suites	2		
Violin Partitas	2	1	VP3
Cello Suites	6		
Totals	29	2	

Thesis of This Chapter

Bach's sarabandes follow the rules of the proportional method, except that the tempo of $\frac{3}{4}$ sarabandes assumes the thirty-second note as shortest note, whether thirty-seconds are present or not. (Note that allemandes make the same assumption about thirty-second notes; see pages 25–30). Table 10.2 groups all twenty-nine sarabandes by time signature, tactus speed, and shortest note ($\frac{3}{4}$ movements lacking thirty-second notes are surrounded by a box).

TABLE 10.2 Bach's sarabandes, grouped by time signature, tactus speed, and shortest note

Time Signature	Tactus Speed	Shortest Note				
		♪	♫	♫ (triplets)	♬	♬
$\frac{3}{4}$	accelerated	CS5	KP2, VP1, CS4		LS2, CS1	KP6
$\frac{3}{4}$	normal	FS1	ES2, FS4	KP3	ES1, ES3, ES4, ES5, FS2, FS3, FS5, FS6, KP4, KP5, FO, VP2, CS2, CS3	KP1
$\frac{3}{2}$	normal		ES6, LS1, CS6			

Note: A box surrounds the eight sarabandes whose tempo departs from the rules of the proportional method, as described in the text.

52 ∞ THE DANCE SUITES

We shall delay our discussion of the KP1 and KP6 sarabandes until page 60 because the presence of sixty-fourth notes in these movements makes them a special case.

> PROPOSITION 1: The tempo of $\frac{3}{4}$ *English Suite* sarabandes assumes the presence of essential thirty-second notes; the tempo of the ES6 sarabande and its double, both of which use the signature $\frac{3}{2}$, assumes the presence of essential sixteenth notes.

In the *English Suites*, all sarabandes (ex. 10.1) and the one sarabande double use the normal tactus. The proportional tempo is 54 BPM[17] for the ES1, ES3, ES4, and ES5 sarabandes, where the beat note is the quarter and the shortest note is the thirty-second (in ES3 and ES5 thirty-second notes appear later in the movement). At 54 BPM these four sarabandes have a solemn musical effect, consistent with contemporaneous descriptions. This tempo is supported by Quantz's statement (see page 50) that the sarabande has the same "movement" as the courante. (We determined earlier (see pages 38–42) that the tempo of normal-tactus courantes is also 54 BPM).

EXAMPLE 10.1 Five of the six *English Suite* sarabandes use the time signature $\frac{3}{4}$; of these five only the sarabande from *English Suite 2* lacks thirty-second notes

A. Sarabande from *English Suite 1* (BWV 806/7); mm. 1–5

B. Sarabande from *English Suite 2* (BWV 807/4); mm. 1–6

C. Sarabande from *English Suite 3* (BWV 808/4); mm. 1–6

---

17   6 thirty-second notes per tactus × 72 BPM ÷ 8 thirty-second notes per quarter note.

EXAMPLE 10.1, cont.

D. Sarabande from *English Suite 4* (BWV 809/4); mm. 1–6

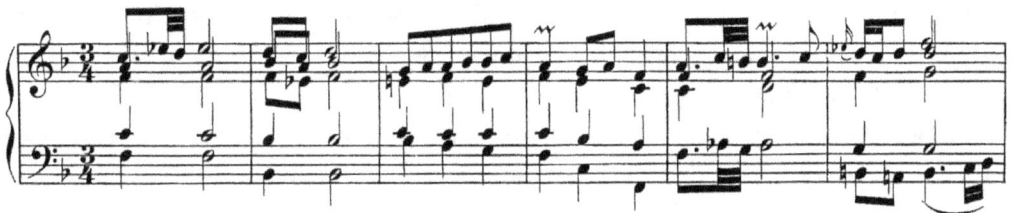

E. Sarabande from *English Suite 5* (BWV 810/4); mm. 1–4

The ES2 sarabande also uses the quarter as beat note, but here the shortest note is the sixteenth (ex. 10.1B, preceding page). Following the ES2 sarabande is an ornamented version of the melody (ex. 10.2), titled Les agréments de la même Sarabande ("The ornaments of the same Sarabande"). The proportional tempo for this melody is 54 BPM because it includes thirty-second notes. This indicates that the tempo for the sarabande itself is 54 BPM because the ornamented melody and the sarabande should have the same tempo. In addition, the proportional tempo for a movement with the sixteenth as shortest note would be 72 BPM.[18] This tempo would lack the appropriately serious musical effect. We conclude that the title Sarabande indicates that, when using the proportional method to determine tempo, we must always assume the thirty-second as shortest note.

EXAMPLE 10.2 Les agréments de la même Sarabande from *English Suite 2* (BWV 807/5) contains thirty-second notes in addition to sixteenth notes; mm. 1–5

---

18 4 sixteenth notes per tactus x 72 BPM ÷ 4 sixteenth notes per quarter note.

A variation also follows the ES3 sarabande (ex. 10.3), this time including the complete texture rather than just the melody. It contains a few ornamental sixty-fourth notes, as well as the expected thirty-second notes. The earliest surviving manuscript,[19] in the handwriting of Bach's student and copyist Bernhard Christian Kayser (1705–1758), shows the time signature **3**. The structure of the measure makes clear that this is shorthand for $\frac{3}{4}$.[20] If the sixty-fourth notes were considered essential, the tempo would be 36 BPM,[21] which is clearly too slow. Also, it would be different from the tempo of the sarabande itself, so the tempo for this movement must be 54 BPM.

EXAMPLE 10.3 Les agréments de la même Sarabande from *English Suite 3* (BWV 808/5) contains a few ornamental sixty-fourth notes; mm. 1–3

The ES6 sarabande (ex. 10.4A) is the only $\frac{3}{2}$ sarabande in the *English Suites*. The beat note is the half and, aside from the cadential elaboration in the next-to-last measure (which includes sixteenths and thirty-seconds), the shortest note is the eighth.

EXAMPLE 10.4 Sarabande and Sarabande Double from *English Suite 6*, where the time signature is $\frac{3}{2}$ and the shortest essential note is the sixteenth

A. Sarabande from *English Suite 6* (BWV 811/4); mm. 1–3 and mm. 23–24

B. Sarabande Double from *English Suite 6* (BWV 811/5); mm. 1–3

---

19 Library Catalog Number: P 1072, Faszikel 2.
20 Kenney, *Proportional Method*, 62.
21 8 sixty-fourth notes per tactus x 72 BPM ÷ 16 sixty-fourth notes per quarter note.

The proportional tempo for a normal-tactus movement in 3/2 with the eighth as shortest note is 54 BPM.[22] This movement sounds rushed at 54 BPM. Further, this is the same tempo as that of the *English Suite* sarabandes using the time signature 3/4. Why would Bach use a different time signature except to specify a different tempo? As cited previously (page 49), the English dance writer Kellom Tomlinson includes two sarabande choreographies in his 1735 dance manual, one using the time signature 3/4 and marked "slow" and one using the time signature 3/2 and marked "very slow." This confirms that a sarabande in 3/2 should be slower than one in 3/4. The next-slower normal-tactus tempo than 54 BPM is 36 BPM,[23] the tempo assuming the sixteenth notes are essential. After that, the next-slower normal-tactus tempo is 27 BPM,[24] the tempo assuming the thirty-second notes are essential. Because this movement sounds wonderful at 36 BPM, and because it is clearly too slow at 27 BPM, we conclude that the tempo of a 3/2 sarabande assumes the presence of essential sixteenth notes.

The tempo is also 36 BPM for the double that follows the ES6 sarabande (ex. 10.4B, preceding page) because the tactus is normal, and because the title Sarabande, when combined with the signature 3/2, indicates that the sixteenth notes in measure 12, though few in number, are essential. As expected, the tempo of the double is the same as that of the sarabande.

PROPOSITION 2: The tempos of later-composed 3/4 sarabandes without sixty-fourth notes assume the presence of thirty-second notes.

The opening measures of the nineteen later 3/4 sarabandes (omitting those with sixty-fourth notes) are given in example 10.5. Seven of the nineteen also lack thirty-second notes (FS1, FS4, KP2, KP3, VP1, CS4, and CS5), but this does not affect tempo, because they obviously share characteristics of the *English Suite* sarabandes. The tempo is 54 BPM[25] for the thirteen normal-tactus movements and 61 BPM[26] for the six accelerated-tactus movements. These tempos result in solemn musical effects, consistent with contemporaneous descriptions.

In preceding chapters, we saw that Bach experimented with tempo in his later allemandes, courantes, and correntes. He used the accelerated tactus in the KP2, CS1, CS4, and CS5 allemandes, in the KP2, FO, and CS5 courantes, and in the VP1, CS1, and CS4 correntes. Using the accelerated tactus for some sarabandes in later-written suites (KP2, LS2, VP1, CS1, CS4, and CS5) parallels his occasional use of it for other later-written dances.

---

22 3 eighth notes per tactus x 72 BPM ÷ 4 eighth notes per half note.
23 4 sixteenth notes per tactus x 72 BPM ÷ 8 sixteenth notes per half note.
24 6 thirty-second notes per tactus x 72 BPM ÷ 16 thirty-second notes per half note.
25 6 thirty-second notes per tactus x 72 BPM ÷ 8 thirty-second notes per quarter note.
26 81 BPM replaces 72 BPM as the tactus speed.

56 ∞ THE DANCE SUITES

EXAMPLE 10.5 The nineteen sarabandes in 3/4 that lack sixty-fourth notes (other than the *English Suite* sarabandes)

A. Sarabande from *French Suite 1* (BWV 812/3) uses the normal tactus; mm. 1–6

B. Sarabande from *French Suite 2* (BWV 813/3) uses the normal tactus; mm. 1–3

C. Sarabande from *French Suite 3* (BWV 814/3) uses the normal tactus; mm. 1–4

D. Sarabande from *French Suite 4* (BWV 815/3) uses the normal tactus; mm. 1–5

E. Sarabande from *French Suite 5* (BWV 816/3) uses the normal tactus; mm. 1–4

F. Sarabande from *French Suite 6* (BWV 817/3) uses the normal tactus; mm. 1–4

EXAMPLE **10.5, cont.**

G. Sarabande from *Keyboard Partita 2* (BWV 826/4) uses the accelerated tactus; mm. 1–3

H. Sarabande from *Keyboard Partita 3* (BWV 827/4) uses the normal tactus; mm. 1–4

I. Sarabande from *Keyboard Partita 4* (BWV 828/5) uses the normal tactus; mm. 1–3

J. Sarabande from *Keyboard Partita 5* (BWV 829/4) uses the normal tactus; mm. 1–4

K. Sarabande from *French Overture* (BWV 831/7) uses the normal tactus; mm. 1–5

EXAMPLE 10.5, cont.

L. Sarabande from *Lute Suite 2* (BWV 997/3) uses the accelerated tactus; mm. 1–4

M. Sarabande from *Violin Partita 1* (BWV 1002/5) uses the accelerated tactus; mm. 1–6

N. Sarabande from *Violin Partita 2* (BWV 1004/3) uses the normal tactus; mm. 1–5

O. Sarabande from *Cello Suite 1* (BWV 1007/4) uses the accelerated tactus; mm. 1–4

P. Sarabande from *Cello Suite 2* (BWV 1008/4) uses the normal tactus; mm. 1–7

Q. Sarabande from *Cello Suite 3* (BWV 1009/4) uses the normal tactus; mm. 1–6

R. Sarabande from *Cello Suite 4* (BWV 1010/4) uses the accelerated tactus; mm. 1–6

S. Sarabande from *Cello Suite 5* (BWV 1011/4) uses the accelerated tactus; mm. 1–6

The double that follows the VP1 sarabande (ex. 10.6) is exceptional because it is not in the same tempo as the sarabande itself. Continuity is achieved by having the eighth notes in the double move at the same speed as the sixteenth notes in the sarabande. (This is because there are three eighth notes per tactus in the double and three sixteenth notes per tactus in the sarabande.) The effect is a doubling of the speed of the notes because the most prevalent note value in the sarabande is the eighth. Because of the change in meter, the double's tempo (81 BPM[27]) is not the same as the sarabande's tempo (61 BPM). (In 3/4 there are four sixteenth notes per beat, while in 9/8 there are three eighth notes per beat.) Only in VP1 does Bach write doubles that have a different tempo from the related dance. He does it with this sarabande double and with the allemanda double. (See page 32 for more information on VP1 and its doubles.)

EXAMPLE 10.6 Sarabande Double from *Violin Partita 1* (BWV 1002/6); mm. 1–4

PROPOSITION 3: The tempo of later-composed 3/2 sarabandes assumes the presence of essential sixteenth notes.

The LS1 and CS6 sarabandes (ex. 10.7) have the same tempo as the ES6 sarabande (36 BPM) because they share its features (time signature 3/2 and the normal tactus speed), and because the title Sarabande indicates that the few sixteenth notes are essential. (Note that the thirty-second notes in LS1 are clearly ornamental, and that two seemingly ornamental sixteenths appear later in CS6.)

EXAMPLE 10.7 The two sarabandes (other than the *English Suite 6* sarabande) where the time signature is 3/2

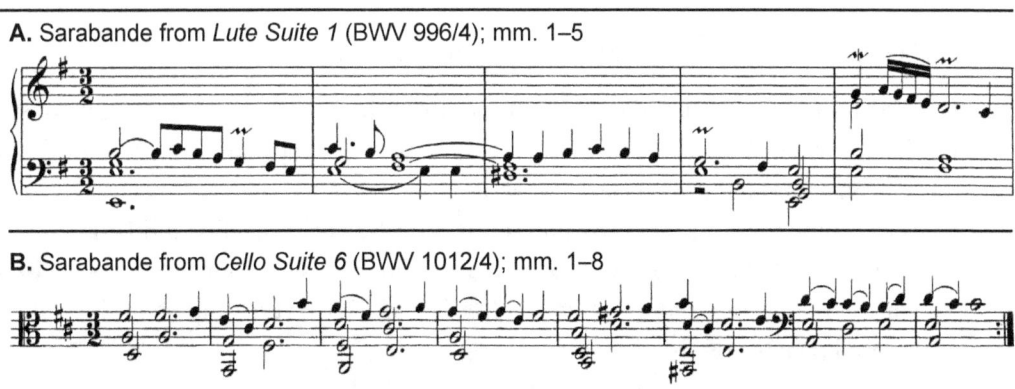

---

27 3 eighth notes per tactus x 81 BPM ÷ 3 eighth notes per dotted quarter note.

PROPOSITION 4: For $\frac{3}{4}$ sarabandes that include sixty-fourth notes, the tempo is 36 BPM for the one using the normal tactus (KP1) and 41 BPM for the one using the accelerated tactus (KP6).

Unlike other $\frac{3}{4}$ sarabandes, KP1 (ex. 10.8A) and KP6 (ex. 10.8B) have the sixty-fourth as shortest note (sixty-fourth notes appear later in both movements). Because KP1 uses the normal tactus, its tempo is 36 BPM,[28] the same tempo as the ES6 sarabande. Because KP6 uses the accelerated tactus,[29] its tempo is 41 BPM (rounded up from 40.5 BPM),[30] one-eighth faster than the ES6 sarabande. This faster tempo is consistent with Bach's tempo experimentation in other later-written dances.

EXAMPLE 10.8 For two sarabandes the shortest note is the sixty-fourth

A. Sarabande from *Keyboard Partita 1* (BWV 825/4) uses the normal tactus; mm. 1–4

B. Sarabande from *Keyboard Partita 6* (BWV 830/5) uses the accelerated tactus; mm. 1–3

Summary

The tempos for Bach's sarabandes are shown in table 10.3.

- The tempo for sarabandes in $\frac{3}{4}$ with no notes shorter than the thirty-second is 54 BPM for the eighteen movements using the normal tactus and 61 BPM for the six movements using the accelerated tactus.
- The tempo for the three sarabandes in $\frac{3}{2}$ is 36 BPM (ES6, CS6, and LS1).
- The tempo for the two sarabandes in $\frac{3}{4}$ that include sixty-fourth notes is 36 BPM for the one using the normal tactus (KP1) and 41 BPM for the one using the accelerated tactus (KP6).

---

28 8 sixty-fourth notes per tactus x 72 BPM ÷ 16 sixty-fourth notes per quarter note.
29 The accelerated tactus was first established in the earlier allemande.
30 81 BPM replaces 72 BPM as the tactus speed.

TABLE 10.3 Bach's sarabandes, grouped by tempo and by beat note

Beat Note	Tempo			
	36 BPM	41 BPM	54 BPM	61 BPM
♩	KP1	KP6	ES1, ES2, ES3, ES4, ES5, FS1, FS2, FS3, FS4, FS5, FS6, KP3, KP4, KP5, FO, CS2, CS3, VP2	KP2, LS2, CS1, CS4, CS5, VP1
♩	ES6, CS6, LS1			

Note: A box surrounds examples of the sarabande having similar features to the prototypical sarabandes found in Bach's *English Suites*.

Further Thoughts

1. Why do some of Bach's sarabandes include no notes shorter than the sixteenth? A hint may be found in the two movements entitled Les agréments de la même Sarabande (ES2 and ES3). They are clearly not intended to be played in addition to the sarabandes themselves. Perhaps they are intended to illustrate ornamentation that Bach found appropriate. Was a performer expected to improvise ornamentation for the sarabande, possibly only on the repeats, so that Bach would only need to provide the longer note values?

2. Of the twenty-two allemandes, courantes, sarabandes, and related doubles in the *English Suites*, twenty use the tempo 54 BPM. Only two are in a different tempo; (the ES6 sarabande and its double use the tempo 36 BPM).

11
Gigas and Gigues

The English word *jig* refers to "a vigorous dance popular in the British Isles from the 16th century onward."[1] An allusion is found in Shakespeare's (1564–1616) *Much Ado about Nothing*, probably written in 1598:

> Wooing, wedding, and repenting
> is as a Scotch jig, a measure,[2] and a cinque-pace:[3]
> > the first suit is hot and hasty like a Scotch jig (and full as fantastical);
> > the wedding, mannerly modest, as a measure, full of state and ancientry;
> > > and then comes Repentance and with his bad legs falls into the cinque-pace faster and faster, till he sink into his grave.[4]

The Old French word *gigue*, the Italian and Spanish *giga*, and the German *Geige* are related, and all refer to "a stringed instrument." The origins of the English word *jig*, however, are uncertain. According to the OED, *jig* is often assumed to be identical with the Old French word *gigue*. The Old French word did not refer to a dance, and it was "obsolete long before the word *jig* is known to have existed." For these reasons, the word *jig* is unlikely to be derived from it. Moreover, the modern French word *gigue*, meaning "a dance, a dance tune" may "have been simply an adoption of the English *jig*." Another possibility is that *jig* is derived from a more modern sense of the French word *giguer*, meaning "to leap, frolic, gambol."[5]

Historical References to the Music for the Gigue

Most seventeenth- and eighteenth-century writers refer to the gigue as a fast movement:

- Georg Muffat (1653–1704), an Alsacian composer and organist, writes in Passau in 1695, "The other pieces, called Gigues and Canaries, must be played the fastest of all, no matter how they are marked."[6]
- Sébastien de Brossard (1655–1730), a French music theorist, in his 1703 dictionary, writes, "*GIGA, GICQUE, GIGUE* (written these three ways by foreigners). An air

---

1 Randel, ed., *The Harvard Dictionary*, 439.
2 The "measures" are stately dances performed at ceremonial occasions in early modern Britain.
3 According to the OED, 415, the "cinque-pace" (pronounced "sink-pace" in English) is "a kind of lively dance much used for some time before and after 1500."
4 Shakespeare, *Much Ado about Nothing*, II, i, 63–69.
5 OED, 1141 & 1509.
6 Wilson, ed., *Georg Muffat*, 17.

usually for instruments, nearly always in triple [compound] meter with numerous dotted notes and syncopations which make it gay and skipping, so to speak."[7]

- Bach's cousin Johann Gottfried Walther (1684–1748), a Thuringian organist, composer, and theorist, writes in 1732 that a "Giga is a piece for instruments; it is a swift English dance, and consists of two repeats in $\frac{3}{8}$, $\frac{6}{8}$ or $\frac{12}{8}$, and it has a dot at the first of each four notes."[8]
- Frederick the Great's court musician Johann Joaquim Quantz (1697–1773) writes in Dresden in 1752, "The *gigue* and the *canarie* have the same tempo. If they are in $\frac{6}{8}$ time, there is a pulse beat on each bar."[9] Given Quantz's estimate of the speed of the human pulse as 80 BPM,[10] the resulting tempo would be 160 BPM, with two dotted-quarter-note beats in the measure.
- In his 1767 *Complete Dictionary of Music* Jean-Jacques Rousseau (1712–1778), the Genevan philosopher, writer, and composer, writes, "GIG. The air of a dance which bears the same name, whose measure is six-eight, and whose movement is lively."[11]
- Daniel Gottlob Türk (1750–1813), a Saxon composer, organist, and Director of Music at Halle University, writes in Leipzig in 1789, "The gigue (giga, gique) is executed in a somewhat short and light fashion. Its character is for the most part one of cheerfulness, and consequently the tempo must be fast. The meters are $\frac{6}{8}$, $\frac{12}{8}$, and even $\frac{3}{8}$."[12]

An exception to the almost-universal description of the Gigue as a fast movement comes from Thomas Mace (c. 1613–1709), an English composer. He writes in London in 1676, "*Toys*, or *Jiggs*, are *Light-Squibbish*[13] *Things*, only fit for *Fantastical*, and *Easie-Light-Headed People*; and are of any sort of time,"[14] implying that not all gigues are fast. The Englishman James Grassineau (born c. 1715) specifically refers to a slow gigue. In his 1740 translation and expansion of Brossard's *Dictionary of Music* (above), he writes in London, "*Giga, Gicque or Gigue*, a jig, some of which are played slow, and others quick, brisk and lively."[15]

An explanation for why Mace and Grassineau do not describe all jigs as being fast may come from the Hamburg composer, lexicographer, diplomat, and music theorist Johann Mattheson (1681–1764), who groups loures, canaries, and gigues together, possibly because all three use compound meter. Perhaps when Mace and Grassineau refer to a slow gigue, they are actually referring to a loure. As Mattheson writes in 1739,

---

7   Brossard, *Dictionary of Music*, 36.
8   Walther, *Musikalisches Lexicon*, 255.
9   Quantz, *On Playing the Flute*, 291.
10 Quantz, *On Playing the Flute*, 288.
11 Rousseau, *A Complete Dictionary of Music*, 185.
12 Türk, *School of Clavier Playing*, 394.
13 According to the OED, 2998, a "squib" is "a common species of firework, in which the burning of the composition is usually terminated by a slight explosion."
14 Mace, *Musick's Monument*, 129.
15 Grassineau, ed., *A Musical Dictionary*, 88.

64 ∞ THE DANCE SUITES

> Something fresh and bright might, in its turn, follow these serious melodies [Mattheson has been discussing the *Entrée*], namely the *Gigue* with its types, which are: the *Loure*, the *Canarie*, the *Giga*. The common or English gigues are characterized by an ardent and fleeting zeal, a rage that soon subsides. On the other hand, the loures or the slow and dotted ones reveal a proud, arrogant nature. For this reason they are very beloved by the Spanish. Canaries must contain great eagerness and swiftness; but still sound a little simple. Finally, the Italian gige, which are not used for dancing, but for fiddling (from which their name might also derive), constrain themselves to extreme speed or volatility; though for the most part in a flowing and uninterrupted manner, like the smoothly flowing current of a brook.[16]

Intriguingly, the German Mattheson appears to associate the English with ardent and fleeting zeal, the Spanish with pride and arrogance, and the Italians with extreme volatility. As interesting as these possible cultural attributes may be, our discussion must be limited to features that affect tempo.

Musicians today recognize two main styles of gigue,

> a fast Baroque dance movement in binary form, the last movement of the mature suite. The details of rhythm and texture vary greatly, deriving from Italian and French models. The Italian giga features triadic, sequential running figures in even note values in $\frac{12}{8}$ at presto tempo. Its texture is mostly homophonic, and phrases are in four-measure units. French versions are less consistent, often having dotted rhythms in duple meter (usually compound, but also simple), syncopations, hemiolas, and cross rhythms. The most influential type opens each strain with imitation and has irregular phrase lengths. Many composers, especially in Germany, mixed elements of the two schools.[17]

Bach's Gigues

Table 11.1 gives the number of gigas, gigues, and gigue doubles in each set of suites. We separate the examples into the French and Italian types identified in *The Harvard Dictionary*, even though the manuscript titles do not always match this identification.

TABLE 11.1 The seven sets of suites in our study and the number of movements in each set, separated by style

	Number of Gigas and Gigues				
Name of Work	Italian-Style Gigas	French-Style Gigues	Movements with Mixed Style	Doubles	Suites That Lack Gigues
English Suites	5		1		
French Suites	4	2			
Keyboard Partitas	4	1			KP2
French Overture		1			
Lute Suites		1	1	1	
Violin Partitas	2				VP1
Cello Suites	5	1			
Totals	20	6	2	1	

---

16 Mattheson, *The Complete Music Director*, 701 [338 in original].
17 Randel, ed., *The Harvard Dictionary*, 351.

Bach's Italian-style gigas employ compound meter, two-voice texture, and a suggestion of perpetual motion achieved through relentless use of the shortest note value. His French-style gigues use dotted rhythms and are written either in compound meter with two-voice texture or in simple meter with three-voice texture. Within these two types, Bach varied the tactus speed, the beat note, and the number of divisions of the beat (table 11.2).

TABLE 11.2 Bach's gigas and gigues, grouped by style of composition, number of divisions of the beat, shortest essential note, and tactus speed

Style of Composition	Beat Note	Divisions of the Beat	Shortest Note	Tactus Speed — Normal	Tactus Speed — Accelerated
Italian: Giga (perpetual motion)	♩.	6	♪	ES1,* ES5, FS3, FS4, FS6, KP5, VP2, VP3, CS2	LS1, LS2,* CS1, CS3, CS6
	♩.	3	♪	ES2, ES3, ES4, KP3	CS4
	♪.	3	♪	ES6, KP4	FS5
	♩	1	♩	KP1	
French: Gigue (dotted rhythms)	♩	8	♪		FS1
	♩	8	♪		KP6
	♩.	6	♪	FO	FS2, CS5

* Note: These two gigas also exhibit the ornamentation and dotted rhythms typical of gigues.

Thesis of This Chapter

The titles Giga and Gigue have the same effect as a fast performance marking such as *Allegro*.

PROPOSITION 1: In Bach's *English Suites*, the title Giga increases the number of shortest notes per tactus.

All six *English Suite* gigas use the normal tactus (ex. 11.1). Two have six divisions of the dotted-quarter-note beat (ES1 and ES5), three have three divisions of the dotted-quarter-note beat (ES2, ES3, and ES4), and one has three divisions of the dotted-eighth-note beat (ES6). All include the consistent use of the shortest note value that is typical of Italian-style gigas. However, most measures of the ES1 giga, including the first three (ex. 11.1A),

66 ∞ THE DANCE SUITES

also exhibit the ornamentation and the dotted rhythms typical of French-style gigues. This movement is an example of the mixed elements mentioned in *The Harvard Dictionary*. We include it among Bach's Italian-style gigas because of its perpetual motion.

EXAMPLE 11.1 The *English Suite* gigas

A. Giga from *English Suite 1* (BWV 806/10); mm. 1–3

B. Giga from *English Suite 2* (BWV 807/8); mm. 1–6

C. Giga from *English Suite 3* (BWV 808/8); mm. 1–4

D. Giga from *English Suite 4* (BWV 809/7); mm. 1–3

E. Giga from *English Suite 5* (BWV 810/7); mm. 1–7

F. Giga from *English Suite 6* (BWV 811/8); mm. 1–3

Without considering the effect of the titles:

- The tempo for ES1 and ES5 (ex. 11.1A and E) would be 48 BPM[18] because the beat note is the dotted quarter, the tactus is normal, and the shortest essential note is the sixteenth. (The numerous thirty-second notes in ES1 are clearly ornamental.)
- The tempo for ES2, ES3, and ES4 (ex. 11.1B, C, and D) would be 72 BPM[19] because the beat note is the dotted quarter, the tactus is normal, and the shortest essential note is the eighth. (The few sixteenth notes that appear later in ES4 are clearly ornamental.)
- The tempo for ES6 (ex. 11.1F) would be 96 BPM[20] because the beat note is the dotted eighth, the tactus is normal, and the shortest note is the sixteenth.

These tempos seem pastoral rather than virtuosic. However, if we accept that Bach's titles Giga and Gigue specify an increase in the number of shortest notes per tactus,[21] the tempos of these movements would be 72 BPM, 96 BPM, and 144 BPM, respectively,[22] providing the energy appropriate for the final movement of a suite.

The *English Suite* gigas, as the earliest written, represent a prototype for Bach's later gigas. We therefore assume that the title in all Bach gigas increases the number of shortest notes per tactus.

> PROPOSITION 2: The title Giga increases the number of shortest notes per tactus in Bach's later suites.

Later in his career, Bach wrote gigas using a variety of beat notes and shortest notes, as he did in the *English Suites*, some using the normal tactus, others using the accelerated tactus. We shall organize our discussion of these later works by the beat note and the number of its divisions. In all examples, the titles increase the number of shortest notes per tactus, providing appropriately virtuosic tempos.

Dotted-Quarter-Note Beat, Six Divisions (twelve survive)

Of the twelve examples, seven use the normal tactus and five use the accelerated tactus (ex. 11.2). All have the dotted quarter as beat note and the sixteenth as shortest note (sixteenths appear later in FS4). The tempo is 72 BPM[23] for those where the tactus is normal and 81 BPM[24] where the tactus is accelerated because the title Giga increases the number of shortest notes per tactus.

---

18 4 sixteenth notes per tactus x 72 BPM ÷ 6 sixteenth notes per dotted quarter note.
19 3 eighth notes per tactus x 72 BPM ÷ 3 eighth notes per dotted quarter note.
20 4 sixteenth notes per tactus x 72 BPM ÷ 3 sixteenth notes per dotted eighth note.
21 Kenney, *Proportional Method*, 78.
22 4 replaces 3, and 6 replaces 4, as the number of shortest notes per tactus.
23 6 (rather than 4) sixteenth notes per tactus x 72 BPM ÷ 6 sixteenth notes per dotted quarter note.
24 81 BPM replaces 72 BPM as the tactus speed.

68 ∞ THE DANCE SUITES

EXAMPLE 11.2 The twelve gigas (other than the gigas from *English Suite 1* and *English Suite 5*) where there are six divisions of the dotted-quarter-note beat

A. Giga from *French Suite 3* (BWV 814/7), where the tactus is normal; mm. 1–7

B. Giga from *French Suite 4* (BWV 815/7), where the tactus is normal; mm. 1–7

C. Giga from *French Suite 6* (BWV 817/8), where the tactus is normal; mm. 1–3

D. Giga from *Keyboard Partita 5* (BWV 829/7), where the tactus is normal; mm. 1–4

E. Giga from *Violin Partita 2* (BWV 1004/4), where the tactus is normal; mm. 1–2

F. Giga from *Violin Partita 3* (BWV 1006/7), where the tactus is normal; mm. 1–3

G. Giga from *Cello Suite 1* (BWV 1007/7), where the tactus is accelerated; mm. 1–7

H. Giga from *Cello Suite 2* (BWV 1008/7), where the tactus is normal; mm. 1–11

EXAMPLE 11.2, cont.

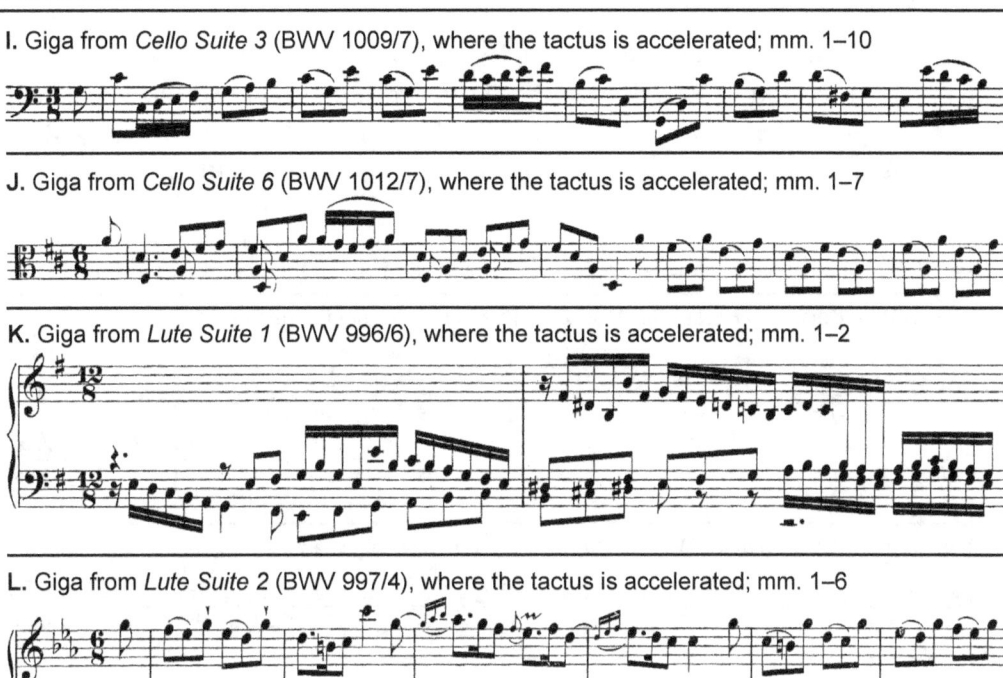

I. Giga from *Cello Suite 3* (BWV 1009/7), where the tactus is accelerated; mm. 1–10

J. Giga from *Cello Suite 6* (BWV 1012/7), where the tactus is accelerated; mm. 1–7

K. Giga from *Lute Suite 1* (BWV 996/6), where the tactus is accelerated; mm. 1–2

L. Giga from *Lute Suite 2* (BWV 997/4), where the tactus is accelerated; mm. 1–6

All these gigas clearly contain elements of the Italian style. The LS2 giga (ex. 11.2L, above), however, is another example of mixed French and Italian elements because twenty-two of its measures (such as measures 2–4) include the dotted rhythms typical of French-style gigues. The tempo of the double (ex. 11.3) that follows the LS2 giga is the same as for the giga itself (81 BPM) because they have the same features. Unlike the LS2 giga, the LS2 double, with its running sixteenth notes, is entirely Italian in style.

EXAMPLE 11.3 Giga Double from *Lute Suite 2* (BWV 997/5); mm. 1–4

Dotted-Quarter-Note Beat, Three Divisions (two survive)

The KP3 (ex. 11.4A) and CS4 (ex. 11.4B) gigas have the dotted quarter as beat note and the eighth as shortest note. Because the title increases the number of shortest notes per tactus, KP3, which uses the normal tactus, has the lively tempo of 96 BPM,[25] and CS4, which uses the accelerated tactus,[26] has the exuberant tempo of 108 BPM.[27]

EXAMPLE 11.4 The two later gigas where there are three divisions of the dotted-quarter-note beat

A. Giga from *Keyboard Partita 3* (BWV 827/7) uses the normal tactus; mm. 1–3

B. Giga from *Cello Suite 4* (BWV 1010/7) uses the accelerated tactus; mm. 1–3

Dotted-Eighth-Note Beat, Three Divisions (two survive)

The KP4 and FS5 gigas (ex. 11.5) both have the dotted eighth as beat note and the sixteenth as shortest note. Because the title increases the number of shortest notes per tactus,

EXAMPLE 11.5 The two later gigas where there are three divisions of the dotted-eighth-note beat

A. Giga from *Keyboard Partita 4* (BWV 828/7) uses the normal tactus; mm. 1–4

B. Giga from *French Suite 5* (BWV 816/7) uses the accelerated tactus; mm. 1–4

---

25 4 (rather than 3) eighth notes per tactus x 72 ÷ 3 eighth notes per dotted quarter note.
26 The accelerated tactus is adopted from the preceding bourrée.
27 81 BPM replaces 72 BPM as the tactus speed.

the tempo of KP4 is 144 BPM[28] since it uses the normal tactus and the tempo of FS5 is 162 BPM[29] since it uses the accelerated tactus.[30]

Special Case

The combination of beat note and shortest note in KP1 (ex. 11.6) does not follow the prototype of the *English Suite* gigues. The time signature is ₵ and the beat note is the quarter. Because the listener's focus is on the quarter notes, rather than on the triplet eighths, the meter seems to be duple. The triplets themselves create a driving perpetual motion that adds elements of compound meter. The title Giga increases the number of quarter notes per tactus from two to three, so the tempo is 216 BPM[31] with the quarter note beat or 108 BPM with the half note beat.

EXAMPLE 11.6 Giga from *Keyboard Partita 1* (BWV 825/7); mm. 1–4

PROPOSITION 3: The title in French-style gigues increases the number of shortest notes per tactus.

The FO, FS2, and CS5 gigues have the dotted quarter as beat note and the sixteenth as shortest note. The FO gigue uses the normal tactus (ex. 11.7A), while the FS2 and CS5 gigues use the accelerated tactus (ex. 11.7B and 11.7C).[32] Because the title Gigue increases the number of shortest notes per tactus, the resulting tempos are 72 BPM and 81 BPM,[33] respectively, appropriate for a finale.

---

28 6 (rather than 4) sixteenth notes per tactus x 72 BPM ÷ 3 sixteenth notes per dotted eighth note.
29 81 BPM replaces 72 BPM as the tactus speed.
30 The accelerated tactus is adopted from the earlier bourrée.
31 3 (rather than 2) quarter notes per tactus x 72 BPM ÷ 1 quarter note per quarter note.
32 In CS5 the accelerated tactus was first established in the eight-movement-previous CS4 bourrée, while in FS2 it was first established in the three-movement-previous air.
33 6 replaces 4 as the number of shortest notes per tactus.

72 ∞ THE DANCE SUITES

EXAMPLE 11.7 The three compound-meter gigues

A. Gigue from *French Overture* (BWV 831/10) uses the normal tactus; mm. 1–3

B. Gigue from *French Suite 2* (BWV 813/7) uses the accelerated tactus; mm. 1–8

C. Gigue from *Cello Suite 5* (BWV 1011/7) uses the accelerated tactus; mm. 1–11

According to *The Harvard Dictionary*, "Gigues written in duple simple meter **may** call for interpretation in triplets."[34] However, Brossard, in his 1703 *Dictionary of Music*, as quoted on page 63, writes that gigues are "**nearly** always in triple [compound] meter,"[35] allowing for the possibility that some gigues are in duple [simple] meter. For reasons presented in our earlier book, we conclude that Bach used simple meter notation for the FS1 and KP6 gigues because he intended that they be played in simple meter.[36]

Bach's two simple-meter gigues exhibit dotted rhythms and use the accelerated tactus.

- The FS1 gigue (ex. 11.8A) uses the time signature ¢ and the thirty-second as shortest note. Because the title Gigue increases the number of thirty-second notes per tactus from six to eight, the tempo is 81 BPM.[37]
- The KP6 gigue (ex. 11.8B) uses the time signature ⏀ and the sixteenth as shortest note (sixteenths appear later in the movement). Because the time signature ⏀ increases the number of sixteenth notes per tactus from four to six,[38] and because the title Gigue further increases the number of sixteenth notes per tactus from six to eight, the tempo is 81 BPM.[39]

Surprisingly, even though their time signatures and shortest notes differ, they have the same tempo.

---

34 Randel, ed., *The Harvard Dictionary*, 351.
35 The emphases are added by the author.
36 Kenney, *Proportional Method*, 78.
37 8 (rather than 6) thirty-second notes per tactus x 81 BPM ÷ 8 thirty-second notes per quarter note.
38 Kenney, *Proportional Method*, 29–30.
39 8 (rather than 4) sixteenth notes per tactus x 81 BPM ÷ 8 sixteenth notes per half note.

EXAMPLE 11.8 The two simple-meter gigues

A. Gigue from *French Suite 1* (BWV 812/6) uses the quarter as beat note; mm. 1–4

B. Gigue from *Keyboard Partita 6* (BWV 830/7) uses the half as beat note; mm. 1–3.

Could the circled three-thirty-second note figures in FS1 (ex. 11.8A, above) be meant to be played as triplets? The three most important eighteenth-century manuscripts do not specify triplets. A review of the alignment of the notes between the two staves in these manuscripts reveals the following:

- The 1722 autograph is a composing score, and the alignment is unclear and inconsistent.[40]
- The 1725 Anna Magdalena Bach copy is mostly aligned as thirty-second notes (that is, two thirty-second notes per sixteenth note).[41]
- A mid-eighteenth-century copy by Bach's student Johann Caspar Vogler is mostly aligned as triplets (that is, three thirty-second notes per sixteenth note).[42]

While the manuscript evidence is inconclusive, more recent editions, including both the BG and the NBA, align the notes as thirty-second notes (two per sixteenth). Because Bach often used a variable dot, one might decide to use thirty-second notes. However, because the piece establishes a clear sixteenth-note plus dotted-eighth-note rhythm at the beginning, it might be more natural to continue that rhythm by using triplets. We invite the reader to try both possibilities.

Summary

Bach wrote two types of gigues, Italian-style gigas with perpetual motion, and French-style gigues with dotted rhythms. Only Italian-style gigas are found in the prototypical *English Suites*. Bach uses various combinations of shortest note, beat note, and tactus speed in his gigas and gigues. In all these movements, the titles Giga and Gigue increase the number of shortest notes per tactus because they act as fast performance markings. The tempos are shown in table 11.3.

---

40 Library Catalog Number: P 224.
41 Library Catalog Number: P 225.
42 Library Catalog Number: P 420.

TABLE 11.3 The tempos of Bach's gigas and gigues, grouped by style of composition, number of divisions of the beat, shortest note, and tactus speed

Style of Composition	Beat Note	Divisions of the Beat	Shortest Note	Tempo	
				Normal Tactus	Accelerated Tactus
Italian: Giga (perpetual motion)	♩.	6	♪	72 BPM: ES1, ES5, FS3, FS4, FS6, KP5, VP2, VP3, CS2	81 BPM: LS1, LS2, CS1, CS3, CS6
	♩.	3	♩	96 BPM: ES2, ES3, ES4, KP3	108 BPM: CS4
	♪.	3	♪	144 BPM: ES6, KP4	162 BPM: FS5
	♩	1	♩	216 BPM: KP1*	
French: Gigue (dotted rhythms)	♩	8	♬		81 BPM: FS1
	♩	8	♪		81 BPM: KP6
	♩.	6	♪	72 BPM: FO	81 BPM: FS2, CS5

* Note: In the KP1 giga three eighth-note triplets are played against each quarter note.

Further Thoughts

1. In ES6, KP1, and KP6, Bach achieves artistic balance by pairing an unusually slow sarabande with an exceptionally fast gigue.

2. Bach's gigas use three different beat notes (the quarter, the dotted eighth, and the dotted quarter), three different shortest notes (the sixteenth, the eighth, and the quarter), and seven different tempos (72, 81, 96, 108, 144, 162, and 216 BPM). Because of this wide variety of meter and tempo it appears that Bach's gigas represent an exploration of ways to achieve rhythmic variety in music of compound meter. (We saw on page 48 that Bach's correntes represent an exploration of ways to achieve rhythmic variety in music of simple-triple meter.)

3. This research indicates that today's performers often play Bach's slow music (such as his sarabandes) too slowly and his moderately fast music (such as his correntes) much too fast. However, they tend to play his fastest gigues not quite fast enough. Of course, Bach was renowned as one of the greatest virtuosos of his time.

12
Movements with Other Titles

All Bach suites include at least one movement other than preludes, allemandes, courantes, sarabandes, and gigues. Bach usually places these movements between the sarabande and gigue, less often either before the sarabande[1] or at the end of the suite.[2] Most of these movements would be called "galanteries" today. However, the LS2 fuga, with its strict counterpoint, and the VP2 chaconne, with its extended form and serious musical effect, are clearly not galanteries.

We shall often refer to the 1789 *School of Clavier Playing* of Daniel Gottlob Türk (1750–1813) because it is a useful source of information about Bach's dance movements, even though it was published thirty-nine years after Bach's death. Türk, a Saxon composer and organist, was Director of Music at Halle University and had studied with one of Bach's former students, Gottfried August Homilius (1714–1785).

Two identically titled movements sometimes appear consecutively, with the Roman numeral I after the first title and the Roman numeral II after the second (for example, the pair of bourrées from *English Suite 1*). Often, but not always, the indication *alternativement* is present. Today, it is customary to play the first dance with repeats followed by the second dance with repeats, and then the first dance again but without repeats. In Bach's day, the word *alternativement* ("alternatively" in English) may have indicated to choose one movement or the other.

Thesis of This Chapter

We expect movements with other titles to follow Bach's proportional method exactly because most, unlike the allemande, courante, sarabande, and gigue, are not derived from long-standing traditions.

Four types of dances (bourrées, gavottes, menuets, and passepieds) appear in the prototypical *English Suites*. Table 12.1 gives, for each set of suites, the number of duple-meter bourrées and gavottes, the number of triple-meter menuets and passepieds, and the number of movements with other titles. We shall first examine movements with each of the dance titles used in the *English Suites*.

---

1 As with the aria from *Keyboard Partita 4*, the air from *Keyboard Partita 6*, the gavottes and passepieds from the *French Overture*, and the fuga from *Lute Suite 2*.
2 As with the capriccio from *Keyboard Partita 2*, the echo from *French Overture*, Tempo di Borea and double from *Violin Partita 1*, and the chaconne from *Violin Partita 2*.

76 ∞ THE DANCE SUITES

TABLE 12.1 The seven sets of suites in our study and the number of additional movements in each set

	Number of Movements by Title					
Name of Work	Bourrée	Gavotte	Menuet	Passepied	Other	Double
English Suites	4	4	2	2		
French Suites	2	3	8		5	
Keyboard Partitas		1	4	1	6	
French Overture	2	2		2	1	
Lute Suites	1				1	
Violin Partitas	2	1	2		2	1
Cello Suites	4	4	4			
Totals	15	15	20	5	15	1

Bourrée

Table 12.2 lists Bach's bourrées, with the information taken from the notation, along with the resulting proportional tempos.

TABLE 12.2 The tempos of Bach's bourrées

			Information Taken from Notation			Results		
Suite	Title	BWV Number	Time Signature	Tactus Speed	Shortest Essential Note	Shortest Notes per Tactus	Beat Note	Tempo (BPM)
ES1	Bourrée I & II	806/8&9	2	normal	♪	4	♩ =	72
ES2	Bourrée I & II	807/6&7	2	normal	♪	4	♩ =	72
FS5	Bourrée	816/5	¢	accelerated	♪	3	♩ =	61
FS6	Bourrée	817/7	2	normal	♪	4	♩ =	72
FO	Bourrée I & II	831/8&9	2	normal	♪	4	♩ =	72
LS1	Bourrée	996/5	¢	accelerated	♪	3	♩ =	61
VP1	Tempo di Borea	1002/7	¢	accelerated	♪	3	♩ =	61
VP3	Bourrée	1006/6	2	normal	♪	4	♩ =	72
CS3	Bourrée I & II	1009/5&6	¢	accelerated	♪	3	♩ =	61
CS4	Bourrée I & II	1010/5&6	¢	accelerated	♪	3	♩ =	61

Türk writes, "The *bourrée* begins with a quarter note upbeat. Its character is somewhat spirited; therefore it must be played at moderate speed and rather lightly."[3] According to the Oxford University Press website www.lexico.com, the French word *bourrée* means "a faggott of twigs" because the *bourrée* was danced around a fire.[4] We have been unsuccessful at finding confirmation of this meaning. Other sources indicate that the French verb *bourrer* means "to fill" or "to stuff" and may refer to excessive alcohol consumption.

The first bourrée from ES1 (ex. 12.1) uses the time signature **2**, the half as beat note, and the eighth as shortest essential note. Because the signature **2** increases the number of eighth notes per tactus from three to four,[5] the tempo is 72 BPM.[6] All *English Suite* bourrées use this tempo because they all have the same features.

EXAMPLE **12.1** Bourrée I from *English Suite 1* (BWV 806/8); mm. 1–6

In Bach's later bourrées, the beat note is still the half, the shortest essential note is still the eighth, and the time signature is either **2** or ¢ (table 12.3). Because those using the signature **2** share the features of the *English Suite* bourrées, they have the same tempo (72 BPM). Those using ¢ have the tempo 61 BPM[7] because the tactus is accelerated; the FS5 bourrée (ex. 12.2, following page) is an example. Surprisingly, normal-tactus bourrées are faster than accelerated-tactus bourrées. This is because, when compared with a movement in **C**, the signature **2** increases tempo by either one-third or one-half,[8] while the signature ¢ increases tempo by only one-eighth.[9]

TABLE **12.3** Bach's bourrées, grouped by time signature

Time Signature	
2	¢
ES1 Bourrée I & II	FS5 Bourrée
ES2 Bourrée I & II	LS1 Bourrée
FS6 Bourrée	VP1 Tempo di Borea
FO Bourrée I & II	CS3 Bourrée I & II
VP3 Bourrée	CS4 Bourrée I & II

---

3   Türk, *School of Clavier Playing*, 393.
4   https://www.lexico.com/en/definition/bourree (accessed March 13, 2020).
5   Kenney, *Proportional Method*, 64–66.
6   4 (rather than 3) eighth notes per tactus x 72 BPM ÷ 4 eighth notes per half note.
7   3 eighth notes per tactus x 81 BPM ÷ 4 eighth notes per half note.
8   4 replaces 3 or 6 replaces 4 as the number of shortest notes per tactus.
9   81 BPM replaces 72 BPM as the tactus speed.

EXAMPLE 12.2 Bourrée from *French Suite 5* (BWV 816/5); mm. 1–3

Tempo di Borea and Double from VP1 (ex. 12.3) deserve special attention because the autograph score[10] and a copy by Anna Magdalena Bach[11] show $\frac{2}{4}$ as the time signature for both movements. The use of $\frac{2}{4}$ as time signature is surprising because it does not reflect the content of the measure. Six of eight eighteenth-century copies also show the time signature $\frac{2}{4}$.[12] However, one copy shows **C** for Tempo di Borea and $\frac{2}{4}$ for its double.[13] The BG and the NBA follow another copy that shows ¢ for both movements.[14] Thus, the manuscript evidence, although weighted toward $\frac{2}{4}$, is inconclusive.

EXAMPLE 12.3 The time signature is uncertain for Tempo di Borea and Double from *Violin Partita 1*

A. Tempo di Borea (BWV 1002/7); mm. 1–5

B. Tempo di Borea Double (BWV 1002/8); mm. 1–5

Note: The *Neue Bach Ausgabe* and the *Bach Gesellschaft* both show the signature ¢, even though the autograph score shows $\frac{2}{4}$.

Because Bach titled this movement Tempo di Borea, one should expect that its tempo would be either 61 BPM or 72 BPM, the tempos of Bach's other bourrées. While neither tempo can be eliminated based on musical taste alone, a performance at 61 BPM yields a more charming musical effect. In the eighteenth-century manuscripts, fifteen of the sixteen time signatures of Tempo di Borea and its double are either $\frac{2}{4}$ or ¢. These two signatures both specify the tempo 61 BPM[15] because the shortest note is the eighth, the beat note is the half, and the tactus is accelerated.[16] The one remaining time signature, which is found in

---

10 Library Catalog Number: P 967.
11 Library Catalog Number: P 268.
12 Library Catalog Numbers: D-B Am.B 70a, D-B Am.B 70b, P573, and P 968.
13 Library Catalog Number: P 267.
14 Library Catalog Number: P 236.
15 3 eighth notes per tactus x 81 BPM ÷ 4 eighth notes per half note.
16 If the time signature were $\frac{2}{4}$ the accelerated tactus would be adopted from the preceding sarabande double.

only one manuscript (**C**), specifies a tempo that is clearly too slow (54 BPM).[17] We accept the editorial choice of the BG and the NBA of the time signature ¢ for these two movements because ¢ specifies the same tempo as does Bach's $\frac{2}{4}$, and because it reflects the content of the measure.

Why did Bach use the time signature $\frac{2}{4}$ even though it does not describe the contents of the measure? We might speculate that Bach used it to emphasize that, in many measures, the quarter note is the beat note.[18]

A further question: why did Bach title this movement Tempo di Borea and not simply Bourrée? The answer may be found in the rhythmic structure at the beginning of the movement. Bourrées usually have constant eighth-note motion, but here much of the motion is in quarter notes. Perhaps Bach wanted to clarify that the tempo and the overall musical effect are that of an accelerated-tactus bourrée.

The Italian word *borea* and the English word *boreas*, meaning "the North Wind," are both derived from the Greek word for North Wind, βορεας. These words seem to be unrelated to the dance bourrée. If the cold North Wind did have something to do with the bourrée, then a tall glass of brandy, and the fire around the faggot of twigs mentioned on page 77, would certainly be of good use.

Gavotte

Table 12.4 lists Bach's gavottes, with the information taken from the notation, along with the resulting proportional tempos.

TABLE 12.4 The tempos of Bach's gavottes

		Information Taken from Notation				Results		
Work	Title	BWV Number	Time Signature	Tactus Speed	Shortest Essential Note	Shortest Notes per Tactus	Beat Note	Tempo (BPM)
ES3	Gavotte I & II	808/6&7	2	normal	♪	4	♩	= 72
ES6	Gavotte I & II	811/6&7	2	normal	♪	4	♩	= 72
FS4	Gavotte	815/4	2	normal	♪	4	♩	= 72
FS5	Gavotte	816/4	¢	accelerated	♪	3	♩	= 61
FS6	Gavotte	817/4	¢	accelerated	♪	3	♩	= 61
KP6	Tempo di Gavotta	830/6	¢	accelerated	♪	3	♩	= 61
FO	Gavotte I & II	831/3&4	2	normal	♪	4	♩	= 72
VP3	Gavotte en Rondeau	1006/3	¢	accelerated	♪	3	♩	= 61

---

17 3 eighth notes per tactus x 72 BPM ÷ 4 eighth notes per half note.
18 Thank you to my piano teacher Don Rankin for this speculation.

TABLE 12.4, cont.

		Information Taken from Notation				Results		
Work	Title	BWV Number	Time Signature	Tactus Speed	Shortest Essential Note	Shortest Notes per Tactus	Beat Note	Tempo (BPM)
CS5	Gavotte I & II	1011/5&6	¢	accelerated	♪	3	𝅗𝅥 =	61
CS6	Gavotte I	1012/5	¢	accelerated	♪	3	𝅗𝅥 =	61
CS6	Gavotte II	1012/6	**2**	normal	♪	4	𝅗𝅥 =	72

Türk writes, "The *gavotte* requires a moderately fast tempo. It begins with an upbeat of two quarters and has a pleasant and rather lively character. From this the manner of execution is easy to decide."[19]

The tempo is 72 BPM[20] for the two ES3 gavottes (ex. 12.4) because the beat note is the half, the shortest note is the eighth, and the time signature **2** increases the number of eighth notes per tactus from three to four. All *English Suite* gavottes use this tempo because they all have the same features.

EXAMPLE 12.4 Gavotte I from *English Suite 3* (BWV 808/6); mm. 1–5

Bach's later gavottes use either **2** or ¢ as time signature and have the eighth as shortest essential note value (table 12.5). Those using the signature **2** share the features of the *English Suite* gavottes and thus have the same tempo (72 BPM). Those using ¢ have the tempo 61 BPM[21] because the tactus is accelerated, the beat note is the half, and the shortest note is the eighth; an example is the FS5 gavotte (ex. 12.5, following page). As with bourrées, accelerated-tactus gavottes are slower than normal-tactus gavottes (see page 77).

---

19   Türk, *School of Clavier Playing*, 394.
20   4 (rather than 3) eighth notes per tactus x 72 BPM ÷ 4 eighth notes per half note.
21   3 eighth notes per tactus x 81 BPM ÷ 4 eighth notes per half note.

Movements with Other Titles ∞ 81

TABLE 12.5 Bach's gavottes, grouped by shortest note and by time signature

Shortest Note	Time Signature			
	2		**¢**	
♪	ES3	Gavotte I & II	FS5	Gavotte
	ES6	Gavotte I & II	FS6	Gavotte
	FS4	Gavotte	KP6	Tempo di Gavotta
	FO	Gavotte I & II	VP3	Gavotte en Rondeau
	CS6	Gavotte II	CS5	Gavotte I & II
			CS6	Gavotte I

EXAMPLE 12.5 Gavotte from *French Suite 5* (BWV 816/4); mm. 1–4

An outlier in both title and rhythmic structure is Tempo di Gavotta from KP6 (ex. 12.6A). As with Tempo di Borea, one should expect that its tempo would be either 61 BPM or 72 BPM, the tempos of Bach's other gavottes. Because the time signature is ¢, the tempo cannot be 72 BPM, so it must be 61 BPM.[22] Thus the beat note is the half and the shortest essential note is the eighth.

EXAMPLE 12.6 Tempo di Gavotta from *Keyboard Partita 6* (BWV 830/6)

Why did Bach title this movement Tempo di Gavotta and not simply Gavotte? Perhaps here, as in Tempo di Borea from VP1, the answer may be found in the rhythmic structure. The many eight note triplets are not unique in a Bach gavotte, since CS5 Gavotte II uses constant triplets. However, numerous measures in this extraordinary piece are clearly

---

22 3 eighth notes per tactus x 81 BPM ÷ 4 eighth notes per half note.

polyrhythmic, where in one voice the beat is divided in three parts, while in the other it is divided in four, as in the circled beats of measures 6 and 7 (ex. 12.6B, preceding page).

Menuet

Table 12.6 lists the menuets in the thirty suites in our study, with the information taken from the notation, along with the resulting proportional tempos.

TABLE 12.6 The tempos of Bach's menuets

			Information Taken from Notation				Results	
Suite	Title	BWV Number	Time Signature	Tactus Speed	Shortest Essential Note	Shortest Notes per Tactus	Beat Note	Tempo (BPM)
ES4	Menuet I & II	809/5&6	**3***	normal	♪	3	♩ = 108	
FS1	Menuet I & II	812/4&5	3/4	normal	♪	3	♩ = 108	
FS2	Menuet I & II	813/5&6	3/4	accelerated	♪	3	♩ = 122	
FS3	Menuet & Trio	814/5&6	3/4	normal	♪	3	♩ = 108	
FS4	Menuet	815/5	3/4	normal	♪	3	♩ = 108	
FS6	Menuet	817/6	3/4	normal	♪	3	♩ = 108	
KP1	Menuet I & II	825/5&6	3/4	normal	♪	3	♩ = 108	
KP4	Menuet	828/6	3/4	normal	♪	3	♩ = 108	
KP5	Tempo di Menuetta	829/5	3/4	normal	♪	3	♩ = 108	
VP3	Menuet I & II	1006/4&5	3/4	accelerated	♪	3	♩ = 122	
CS1	Menuet I & II	1007/5&6	3/4	accelerated	♪	3	♩ = 122	
CS2	Menuet I & II	1008/5&6	3/4	normal	♪	3	♩ = 108	

* Note: The signature **3** is not in Bach's handwriting.

Türk writes, "The *minuet (menuett, minuetto)*, a well-known dance of noble and charming character, is played moderately fast and [agreeably], but executed without embellishments (In some regions the minuet is played much too fast when it is not used for the dance)."[23]

Bach's autograph of Menuet I from ES4 (ex. 12.7) does not survive. The earliest surviving manuscript of this piece, in the handwriting of Bach's student and copyist Bernhard Christian Kayser (1705–1758),[24] shows the time signature **3**, which is equivalent to the

---

23 Türk, *School of Clavier Playing*, 395.
24 Library Catalog Number: P 1072, Faszikel 2.

time signature $\mathbf{\frac{3}{4}}$.[25] The tempo is 108 BPM[26] because the tactus is normal and the shortest essential note is the eighth. As expected, Menuet II has the same tempo because it shares the features of Menuet I.

EXAMPLE 12.7 Menuet I from *English Suite 4* (BWV 809/5); mm. 1–6

In all of Bach's later menuets, the beat note remains the quarter and the shortest essential note remains the eighth. Some use the normal tactus and some use the accelerated tactus (table 12.7). Because those with the normal tactus share the features of the *English Suite* menuets, they have the same tempo (108 BPM). Those with the accelerated tactus[27] have the tempo 122 BPM;[28] an example is the first menuet from FS2 (ex. 12.8).

TABLE 12.7 Bach's menuets, grouped by tactus speed

Tactus Speed	
Normal	Accelerated
ES4 Menuet I & II	FS2 Menuet I & II
FS1 Menuet I & II	VP3 Menuet I & II
FS3 Menuet & Trio	CS1 Menuet I & II
FS4 Menuet	
FS6 Menuet	
KP1 Menuet I & II	
KP4 Menuet	
KP5 Tempo di Menuetta	
CS2 Menuet I & II	

EXAMPLE 12.8 Menuet I from *French Suite 2* (BWV 813/5); mm. 1–6

---

25 Kenney, *Proportional Method*, 62.
26 3 eighth notes per tactus x 72 BPM ÷ 2 eighth notes per quarter note.
27 The accelerated tactus for the FS2 menuets was established in the preceding air, for the VP3 menuets it was established in the preceding gavotte, and for the CS1 menuets it was established in the earlier allemande.
28 81 BPM replaces 72 BPM as the tactus speed.

84 ∞ THE DANCE SUITES

Tempo di Menuetta from KP5 (ex. 12.9) deserves extra scrutiny because Bach titled the movement Tempo di Menuetta, rather than simply Menuet. The tempo is 108 BPM because the tactus is normal, the beat note is the quarter, and the shortest essential note is the eighth. Although this movement has the same tempo as Bach's other normal-tactus menuets, it is not heard as an ordinary menuet because its double stems group the notes in threes in thirty-eight of its fifty-two measures (as in measures 1–3 and measures 5–7). Only at cadences are the eighths grouped in twos (as they are in the typical menuet). These cadences are heard as hemiolas (as in measure 4).

EXAMPLE 12.9 Tempo di Menuetta from *Keyboard Partita 5* (BWV 829/5); mm. 1–7

Passepied

Table 12.8 lists Bach's passepieds, with the information taken from the notation, along with the resulting proportional tempo.

TABLE 12.8 The tempo of Bach's passepieds

			Information Taken from Notation			Results		
Suite	Title	BWV Number	Time Signature	Tactus Speed	Shortest Essential Note	Shortest Notes per Tactus	Beat Note	Tempo (BPM)
ES5	Passepied I & II	810/5&6	3/8	normal	♪	4	♪ =	144
KP5	Passepied	829/6	3/8	normal	♪	4	♪ =	144
FO	Passepied I & II	831/5&6	3/8	normal	♪	4	♪ =	144

Türk writes, "The *passepied* is a French dance which has much in common with the minuet. Its character is also noble but somewhat livelier than the minuet; therefore the tempo must be a little faster and the execution somewhat lighter."[29] Türk's reference to lighter execution is consistent with Kirnberger's statement that shorter note values are played more lightly than longer ones,[30] indicating that the (shorter) sixteenth notes in Bach's passepieds would be lighter than the (longer) eighth notes in Bach's menuets.

---

29 Türk, *School of Clavier Playing*, 395.
30 Kenney, *Proportional Method*, 48.

The earliest of Bach's passepieds are the two from ES5 (ex. 12.10). The tempo is 144 BPM[31] because the time signature is $\frac{3}{8}$, the tactus is normal, the beat note is the eighth, and the shortest note is the sixteenth. Bach's other passepieds share these features and therefore have the same tempo.

EXAMPLE 12.10 Passepied I from *English Suite 5* (BWV 810/5); mm. 1–8

Additional Titles

Table 12.9 lists these fifteen movements, with the information taken from the notation, along with the resulting proportional tempos.

TABLE 12.9 The tempos of Bach's additional dance movements, other than the bourrée, the gavotte, the menuet, and the passepied

			Information Taken from Notation			Results		
Title	Suite	BWV Number	Time Signature	Tactus Speed	Shortest Essential Note	Shortest Notes per Tactus	Beat Note	Tempo (BPM)
Air	FS2	813/4	₵	accelerated	♪	4	♩ =	81
Air	FS4	815/6	C	normal	♪	4	♩ =	72
Air	KP6	830/4	₵	accelerated	♪	3	𝅗𝅥 =	61
Anglaise	FS3	814/4	2	normal	♪	4	𝅗𝅥 =	72
Aria	KP4	828/4	2/4	normal	♪	4	♩ =	72
Burlesca	KP3	827/5	3/4	normal	♪	4	♩ =	72
Capriccio	KP2	826/6	2/4	accelerated	♪	4	♩ =	81
Chaconne	VP2	1004/5	6/4	normal	♪	6	𝅗𝅥 =	54
Echo	FO	831/11	2/4	normal	♪	4	♩ =	72

---

31 4 sixteenth notes per tactus x 72 BPM ÷ 2 sixteenth notes per eighth note.

TABLE 12.9, cont.

Title	Suite	BWV Number	Time Signature	Tactus Speed	Shortest Essential Note	Shortest Notes per Tactus	Beat Note		Tempo (BPM)
Fuga	LS2	997/2	6/8	accelerated	♪	4	♩.	=	54
Loure	FS5	816/6	6/4	accelerated	♪	4	♩	=	81
Loure	VP3	1006/2	6/4	normal	♪	4	♩	=	72
Polonaise	FS6	817/5	3/4	accelerated	♪	4	♩	=	81
Rondeaux	KP2	826/5	3/8	accelerated	♪	4	♩.	=	54
Scherzo	KP3	827/6	2/4	normal	♪	4	♩	=	72

Air or Aria

According to *The Harvard Dictionary*, "In Baroque suites, the practice of transcribing operatic airs resulted in the use of the title [Air] for newly composed tuneful movements that did not fit any dance category."[32] Because of their varying features, each of the movements titled Air uses a different tempo. This is not surprising because the title itself, meaning "a tune," cannot carry information about tempo.

- The tempo is 61 BPM[33] for the KP6 air (ex. 12.11A) because the beat note is the half, the shortest essential note is the eighth, and the time signature ¢ establishes the accelerated tactus.
- The tempo is 72 BPM[34] for the FS4 air (ex. 12.11B) because the tactus is normal, the beat note is the quarter, and the shortest note is the sixteenth. The KP4 aria (ex. 12.11C) has the same tempo.
- The tempo is 81 BPM[35] for the FS2 air (ex. 12.11D) because the time signature is ¢, the beat note is the quarter, and the shortest note is the sixteenth.

Why did Bach not title the KP6 air Gavotte? Although it has a texture similar to that of Bach's gavottes, and it also has the gavotte's distinctive half-measure pickup, its musical effect is serious rather than pleasant and lively. Or could it be a "transcribed operatic air?"

---

32 Randel, ed., *The Harvard Dictionary*, 29.
33 3 eighth notes per tactus x 81 BPM ÷ 4 eighth notes per half note.
34 4 sixteenth notes per tactus x 72 BPM ÷ 4 sixteenth notes per quarter note.
35 81 BPM replaces 72 BPM as the tactus speed.

EXAMPLE 12.11 Bach movements titled "Air" or "Aria" use a variety of features

A. In Air from *Keyboard Partita 6* (BWV 830/4), the time signature is ₵ and the shortest note is the eighth; mm. 1–4

B. In Air from *French Suite 4* (BWV 815/6), the time signature is C and the shortest note is the sixteenth; mm. 1–2

C. In Aria from *Keyboard Partita 4* (BWV 828/4), the time signature is 2/4 and the shortest note is the sixteenth; mm. 1–7

D. In Air from *French Suite 2* (BWV 813/4), the time signature is ₵ and the shortest note is the sixteenth; mm. 1–2

Anglaise

According to Türk, "The *Anglaise* (English dance, *contredanse*,[36] country dance) is for the most part of a very spirited character which often borders on the moderately comic. It is played in a very lively, almost skipping manner. The first note of every measure is strongly accented. Although the tempo is fast, it is not always of the same degree of speed."[37]

The tempo is 72 BPM[38] for the FS3 anglaise (ex. 12.12) because the beat note is the half, the shortest note is the eighth, and the time signature **2** increases the number of eighth notes per tactus from three to four. This anglaise is similar in texture to Bach's gavottes but lacks the half-measure pickup.

---

36 According to the OED, 541, the French word *contredanse* is a corruption of the English phrase "country dance," suggested by the arrangement of the dancers in two opposite lines.
37 Türk, *School of Clavier Playing*, 393.
38 4 (rather than 3) eighth notes per tactus x 72 BPM ÷ 4 eighth notes per half note.

88 ∞ THE DANCE SUITES

EXAMPLE 12.12 Anglaise from *French Suite 3* (BWV 814/4); mm. 1–5

Burlesca

A burlesca is "a playful or comical piece."[39] The French word *burlesque* is derived from the Italian word *burla*, meaning ridicule or mockery.[40] Bach would have been familiar with the use of the term *burlesca* to refer to caricature or parody in literary, dramatic, and musical works. He might have been surprised, however, at the more modern burlesque, which was popular in cabarets in the United States in the late-nineteenth and early-twentieth centuries, and which featured bawdy humor and striptease.

The tempo is 72 BPM[41] for the KP3 burlesca (ex. 12.13) because the time signature is $\frac{3}{4}$, the tactus is normal, the beat note is the quarter, and the shortest essential note is the sixteenth.

EXAMPLE 12.13 Burlesca from *Keyboard Partita 3* (BWV 827/5); mm. 1–4

Capriccio

The capriccio is "a humorous, fanciful, or bizarre composition, often characterized by an idiosyncratic departure from current stylistic norms. Throughout its history the capriccio has been closely allied with pieces called fantasia, but more extreme in contrasts and more daring in deviating from conventions of harmony and counterpoint."[42]

For the KP2 capriccio, the tempo is 81 BPM[43] (ex. 12.14) because the time signature is $\frac{2}{4}$, the tactus is accelerated,[44] the beat note is the quarter, and the shortest note is the sixteenth. This movement is structured as a strictly written three-voice fugue, although presented with an accompanied subject (the accompaniment adds a driving motion to the

---

39 Randel, ed., *The Harvard Dictionary*, 125.
40 OED, 298.
41 4 sixteenth notes per tactus x 72 BPM ÷ 4 sixteenth notes per quarter note.
42 Randel, ed., *The Harvard Dictionary*, 148.
43 4 sixteenth notes per tactus x 81 BPM ÷ 4 sixteenth notes per quarter note.
44 The accelerated tactus was established in the earlier allemande.

piece and clarifies the meter). In addition, the form is binary, rather than through-composed. Perhaps these features dissuaded Bach from using the title Fugue. And perhaps he chose the title Capriccio because of the unusual melodic leaps of tenths and elevenths (as in measure 3), which certainly depart from then-current stylistic norms.

EXAMPLE 12.14 Capriccio from *Keyboard Partita 2* (BWV 826/6); mm. 1–5

Chaconne

According to Türk, "The *ciaconne (chaconne, ciaccona)* is a composition of moderately fast tempo in $\frac{3}{4}$ measure. Every first note of a measure is rather strongly marked. Composers are accustomed to repeat the basic melody of this dance composition but always in a somewhat varied form."[45] *The Harvard Dictionary* adds that the chaconne is "a continuous variation form of the Baroque, similar to the passacaglia, based on the chord progression of a late 16th-century dance imported into Spain and Italy from Latin America," and that the French chaconne was "rather more sedate than its southern counterpart."[46]

The tempo is 54 BPM[47] for the VP2 chaconne (ex. 12.15) because the time signature is $\frac{3}{4}$, the tactus is normal, the beat note is the quarter, and the shortest note is the thirty-second. The first sixteen variations are in D minor and are followed by a four-measure coda. The mode then shifts to D major for nine variations and a second coda. The piece then returns to D minor for five variations and a restatement of the theme. We are not aware of any other Bach movement with the half-note quarter-note harmonic rhythm (surrounded by an oval in ex. 12.15) exhibited in this extraordinary piece.

EXAMPLE 12.15 Chaconne from *Violin Partita 2* (BWV 1004/5); mm. 1–10

---

45 Türk, *School of Clavier Playing*, 394.
46 Randel, ed., *The Harvard Dictionary*, 155–156.
47 6 thirty-second notes per tactus x 72 BPM ÷ 8 thirty-second notes per quarter note.

Echo

The Harvard Dictionary defines *echo* as "the acoustical phenomenon in which a sound is heard as having been repeated, usually from some distance, because of the reflection of the sound waves back toward the listener from some, often distant, surface." The dictionary also states that *echo* is "a musical effect that imitates the acoustical phenomenon."[48]

For the FO echo, the tempo is 72 BPM[49] (ex. 12.16) because the time signature is $\frac{2}{4}$, the tactus speed is normal, the beat note is the quarter, and the shortest note is the sixteenth. Bach undoubtedly titled this piece Echo because of the alternating *piano* and *forte* indicated at fourteen points in the piece, such as at measure 5. The figure D C# B at the beginning of measure 5 (circled in ex. 12.16) represents an echo of the falling third D B at the end of measure 4, which is presumed to be *forte*.

EXAMPLE 12.16 Echo from *French Overture* (BWV 831/11); mm. 1–6

Fuga

The strictly written contrapuntal structure of the LS2 fuga sets it apart from the other movements in this chapter. Its tempo is 54 BPM[50] because the time signature is $\frac{6}{8}$, the tactus is accelerated,[51] the beat note is the dotted quarter, and the shortest note is the sixteenth (ex. 12.17).

EXAMPLE 12.17 Fuga from *Lute Suite 2* (BWV 997/2); mm. 1–5

Loure

According to Türk, "The *loure* is performed with strength, slowly, and seriously. The dotted notes should not be played in a detached manner. These compositions generally begin with an eighth [followed by a] quarter note as an upbeat, although this is not always

---

48   Randel, ed., *The Harvard Dictionary*, 270.
49   4 sixteenth notes per tactus x 72 BPM ÷ 4 sixteenth notes per quarter note.
50   4 sixteenth notes per tactus x 81 BPM ÷ 6 sixteenth notes per dotted quarter note.
51   The accelerated tactus was established in the suite's opening prelude.

the case. Mattheson calls the loure a type of slow gigue."[52] The tempo is 72 BPM[53] for the VP3 loure (ex. 12.18) because the time signature is $\frac{6}{4}$, the tactus is normal, the beat note is the quarter, and the shortest note is the sixteenth. The tempo is 81 BPM[54] for Bach's other loure, from FS5 (not shown), because the tactus is accelerated.[55]

EXAMPLE 12.18 Loure from *Violin Partita 3* (BWV 1006/2); mm. 1–4

Polonaise

Türk writes that "the *polonaise* is a Polish national dance of a solemn and ceremonious character. The tempo of the true polonaise . . . is faster than we generally take it."[56] The tempo for the FS6 polonaise is 81 BPM[57] (ex. 12.19) because the time signature is $\frac{3}{4}$, the tactus is accelerated,[58] the beat note is the quarter, and the shortest note is the sixteenth.

EXAMPLE 12.19 Polonaise from *French Suite 6* (BWV 817/5); mm. 1–5

Rondeaux

The Harvard Dictionary states that "in the Baroque era, [the rondeau was] a simple refrain form, usually employed in dance movements. The term is sometimes used alone as a title but does not have implications of tempo, meter, or texture."[59]

The tempo for the KP2 rondeaux (ex. 12.20) is 54 BPM[60] because the time signature is $\frac{3}{8}$, the tactus is accelerated,[61] the shortest note is the sixteenth, and the beat note is the dotted quarter. The title Rondeaux refers to the structure, where a sixteen-measure refrain occurs four times in the movement. We speculate that Bach used the plural form of the term because melodic details of the refrain vary at each appearance.

---

52 Türk, *School of Clavier Playing*, 395.
53 4 sixteenth notes per tactus x 72 BPM ÷ 4 sixteenth notes per quarter note.
54 81 BPM replaces 72 BPM as the tactus speed.
55 The accelerated tactus was established in the preceding bourrée.
56 Türk, *School of Clavier Playing*, 396.
57 4 sixteenth notes per tactus x 81 BPM ÷ 4 sixteenth notes per quarter note.
58 The accelerated tactus was established in the preceding gavotte.
59 Randel, ed., *The Harvard Dictionary*, 741.
60 4 sixteenth notes per tactus x 81 BPM ÷ 6 sixteenth notes per dotted quarter note.
61 The accelerated tactus was established in the earlier allemande.

EXAMPLE 12.20 Rondeaux from *Keyboard Partita 2* (BWV 826/5); mm. 1–8

Scherzo

The English word *scherzo* derives from the Italian word *scherzare*, meaning to sport [joke] or to play.[62] *The Harvard Dictionary* states, "In the 18th century [a scherzo was] one movement of a suite or other multimovement work, quick in tempo and light in style."[63]

The tempo is 72 BPM for the KP3 scherzo (ex. 12.21) because the time signature is $\frac{2}{4}$, the tactus is normal, the beat note is the quarter, and the shortest note is the sixteenth. In the early- to mid-eighteenth century, a scherzo was often in $\frac{2}{4}$. From the late-eighteenth century on, scherzos were usually in a quick $\frac{3}{4}$, felt in one beat per measure.

EXAMPLE 12.21 Scherzo from *Keyboard Partita 3* (BWV 827/6); mm. 1–4

Summary

- Every Bach suite includes at least one movement other than preludes, allemandes, courantes, sarabandes, and gigues.
- In the prototypical *English Suites*, the additional movements are limited to the duple-meter bourrée and gavotte and the triple-meter menuet and passepied.
- In his later suites, Bach included forty-three movements having these same four titles. He also included fifteen movements having titles different from these four, eight in duple meter and seven in triple.
- The tempos of all these movements follow the rules of the proportional method exactly, unaffected by their titles.

---

62 OED, 2664.
63 Randel, ed., *The Harvard Dictionary*, 761.

Appendix—Overview of Bach's Dance Music

We list all the dance movements from the thirty suites in our study in tables A.1 and A.2. We exclude movements not derived from dance traditions, such as the LS2 fuga and non-allemande introductory movements.

The tempos in BPM of Bach's music may be expressed in two ways, depending on the choice of a longer or shorter note as beat note.[1] In both tables, parentheses are placed around tempos too slow or too fast to be easily felt.

Table A.1 lists all sixty-eight dance movements using simple-duple meter. In these movements, the longer possible beat note is the half, and the shorter possible beat note is the quarter. The table shows both expressions of tempo, along with Bach's titles and the number of movements using each combination of tempo and title. Bach uses nine different tempos and twelve different titles for these simple-duple-meter movements.

Combinations above the box in table A.1 would be too slow if the half note were used as the beat note. Combinations below the box would be too fast if a quarter-note beat were used. The box itself surrounds those that may be felt with either a half-note or a quarter-note beat.

TABLE A.1 The number of simple-duple-meter dance movements, by combination of tempo and title; parentheses surround tempos which are theoretical but not practical

Normal Tactus				Accelerated Tactus			
Tempo of Half Note (BPM)	Tempo of Quarter Note (BPM)	Title	Number of Examples	Tempo of Half Note (BPM)	Tempo of Quarter Note (BPM)	Title	Number of Examples
(18)	36	Allemanda	2	(20)	41		none
(27)	54	Allemande	21	(30)	61	Allemande	4
36	72	Air	1	41	81	Air	1
		Aria	1			Capriccio	1
		Echo	1			Gigue	1
		Scherzo	1				
54	108		none	61	122	Air	1
						Bourrée	7
						Gavotte	7
72	(144)	Anglaise	1	81	(162)	Gigue	1
		Bourrée	8				
		Gavotte	8				
* 108	(216)	Giga	1				

* Note: The KP1 giga also includes eighth-note triplets on each quarter note.

---

1   Kenney, *Proportional Method*, 26–28.

Table A.2 lists the 114 movements that use either compound meter or simple-triple meter. Here, too, each tempo is expressed in two ways, by choosing either a dotted note as beat note (compound meter) or a note that is one-third as long as the dotted note as beat note (simple meter). The table shows both expressions of tempo, along with Bach's titles and the number of movements using each combination of tempo and title. Bach uses sixteen different tempos and twelve different titles for these movements.

TABLE A.2 The number of compound-meter and simple-triple-meter dance movements, by combination of tempo and title; parentheses surround tempos that are theoretical but not practical

Normal Tactus				Accelerated Tactus			
Tempo as Compound Meter (BPM)	Tempo as Simple Meter (BPM)	Title	Number of Examples	Tempo as Compound Meter (BPM)	Tempo as Simple Meter (BPM)	Title	Number of Examples
(12)	36	Sarabande	4	(14)	41	Sarabande	1
(18)	54	Courante	10	(20)	61	Courante	3
		Sarabande	18			Sarabande	6
		Chaconne	1				
(24)	72	Corrente	8	(27)	81	Corrente	2
		Loure	1			Loure	1
		Burlesca	1			Polonaise	1
36	108	Courante	1	41	122	Corrente	1
		Corrente	3			Menuet	6
		Menuet	14				
48	144	Corrente	1	54	162	Rondeaux	1
		Passepied	5				
72	(216)	Giga	9	81	(243)	Giga	4
		Gigue	1			Gigue	3
96	(288)	Giga	4	108	(324)	Giga	4
144	(432)	Giga	2	162	(486)	Giga	1

Note: A box surrounds tempo combinations that can be heard as either compound meter or simple-triple meter.

Combinations above the box in table A.2 would be too slow to be felt as compound meter, so they must be heard as simple. Combinations below the box would be too fast to be felt as simple meter, so they must be heard as compound. The box itself surrounds tempo combinations that can be heard as either simple-triple meter or compound meter. This table shows that triple meter movements are part of a continuum, ranging from slow (simple meter) to fast (compound meter).

Almost every combination of meter and tempo that was available to Bach in his proportional method is represented in these two tables. The two exceptions, indicated by the word *none* in table A.1, are that no duple-meter dance movements survive using the tempo 54 BPM to the half-note beat, and none using the tempo 41 BPM to the quarter-note beat. These movements span his entire career and show that Bach maximized variety in meter and tempo.

Bibliography

Arbeau, Thoinot. *Orchésographie*. Translated by Mary Stewart Evans. Mineola: Dover Publications, 2011.

Bach, Johann Sebastian. *Johann Sebastian Bach's Werke*. Edited under the auspices of the *Bach Gesellschaft* in Leipzig. Leipzig: Breitkopf & Härtel, 1851–1900.

Bach, Johann Sebastian. *Neue Ausgabe Sämtlicher Werke*. Edited under the auspices of the Johann-Sebastian-Bach-Institut Göttingen and the Bach-Archiv Leipzig. Kassel: Bärenreiter, 1954–.

de Brossard, Sébastien. *Dictionary of Music*. Translated and edited by Albion Gruber. Ottawa: Institute of Medieval Music, 1982.

de Cervantes, Miguel. *Entremeses*. Edited by Alberto Castilla. Madrid: Impreso en Lavel, S. A. Humanes, 2007.

David, Hans T. and Arthur Mendel, eds. *The New Bach Reader*. Revised by Christoph Wolff. New York: Norton & Co., 1998.

Froberger, Johann Jacob. *Libro secondo di toccate, etc.*, alla sac.a Caes.a M.ta diuotissim:te dedicato in Vienna li 29 Settembre Ao. 1649.

Gorce, Jérôme de La. *Jean-Baptiste Lully*. Paris: Librairie Arthème Fayard, 2002.

Grassineau, James, ed. and trans. *A Musical Dictionary by Sébastien de Brossard*. London: for J. Wilcox, 1740. ECCO Print Edition.

Kenney, Leslie M. *The Tempo Implications of Bach's Notation: Part 1—The Proportional Method*. Saunderstown, RI: WTB Press, 2021.

Kirnberger, Johann Philipp. *The Art of Strict Musical Composition*. Translated by David Beach and Jurgen Thym. New Haven: Yale University Press, 1982.

Little, Meredith, and Natalie Jenne. *Dance and the Music of J. S. Bach*. Expanded edition. Bloomington: Indiana University Press, 2001.

Mace, Thomas. *Musick's Monument*. 2nd ed., vol. I. Paris: Éditions du Centre National de la Recherche Scientifique, 1966.

de Mariana, Juan. "Tratado contra los juegos públicos." In *Obras del Padre Juan de Mariana*, vol. XXXI of *Biblioteca de Autores Hispaneolas*. Madrid: Ediciones Atlas, 1950.

Marino, Giambattista. *L'Adone*. Accessed on August 15, 2020 at https://it.wikisource.org/wiki/Adone.

Mattheson, Johann. *Der Vollkommenen Capellmeister*. Edited by Friederike Ramm. Kassel: Bärenreiter, 1999. Also, Mattheson, Johann. *Der Vollkommenen Capellmeister*. Translated by Ernest C. Harriss. Ann Arbor: UMI Research Press, 1981.

Muffat, Georg. *Florilegium Primum*, in *Denkmäler der Tonkunst Österreich*, vol. I. Vienna: Artaria & Co., 1895.

Muffat, Georg. *Florilegium Secundum*, in *Denkmäler der Tonkunst Österreich*, vol. II. Vienna: Artaria & Co., 1895.

Muffat, Georg. *On Performance Practice*. Edited by David K. Wilson. Bloomington: Indiana University Press, 2001.

Oxford English Dictionary, The Compact Edition. Oxford: Oxford University Press, 1971.

Praetorius, Michael. *Syntagma Musicum III*. Translated by Jeffery T. Kite-Powell. Oxford: Oxford University Press, 2004.

Quantz, Johann Joachim. *On Playing the Flute*, 2nd ed. Translated by Edward R. Reilly. New York: Schirmer, 1985.

Rameau, Pierre. *The Dancing Master*. Translated by Cyril W. Beaumont. Alton: Dance Books, 2003.

Randel, Don Michael, ed. *The Harvard Dictionary of Music*, 4th ed. Cambridge: Belknap Press, 2003.

Rousseau, Jean-Jacques. *A Complete Dictionary of Music*. Translated by William Waring, 2nd edition. London: J. Murray, 1779. ECCO Print Editions

Sadie, Stanley and John Tyrrell, eds. *The New Grove Dictionary of Music and Musicians*, 2nd ed., 29 vols. London: Macmillan, 2001.

Shakespeare, William. *Much Ado about Nothing*. Edited by Josephine Waters Bennett. New York: Penguin Books, 1971.

Stevenson, Robert. "The First Dated Mention of the Sarabande." *Journal of the American Musicological Society* (1952) 5 (1): 29–31.

Tomlinson, Kellom. *The Art of Dancing*. Hampshire: Noverre Press, 2010.

Türk, Daniel Gottlob. *School of Clavier Playing*. Translated by Raymond H. Haggh. Lincoln: University of Nebraska Press, 1982.

Walther, Johann Gottfried. *Musikalisches Lexikon oder Musicalische Bibliothec*. Edited by Friederike Ramm. Kassel: Bärenreiter, 2001.

Index of Cited Bach Works

BWV Number	Title	Page(s)
806–811	*English Suites*	5
806/1	Prelude from *English Suite 1*	9
806/2	Allemande from *English Suite 1*	28
806/3	Courante I from *English Suite 1*	43, 48
806/4	Courante II from *English Suite 1*	44
806/5	Courante II Double I from *English Suite 1*	45
806/6	Courante II Double II from *English Suite 1*	45
806/7	Sarabande from *English Suite 1*	59
806/8	Bourrée I from *English Suite 1*	74
806/10	Giga from *English Suite 1*	90
807/1	Prelude from *English Suite 2*	10
807/2	Allemande from *English Suite 2*	28
807/3	Courante from *English Suite 2*	44
807/4	Sarabande from *English Suite 2*	59
807/5	Les agréments de la même Sarabande from *English Suite 2*	60
807/8	Giga from *English Suite 2*	91
808/1	Prelude from *English Suite 3*	11
808/2	Allemande from *English Suite 3*	29
808/3	Courante from *English Suite 3*	44
808/4	Sarabande from *English Suite 3*	59
808/5	Les agréments de la même Sarabande from *English Suite 3*	61
808/6	Gavotte I from *English Suite 1*	77
808/8	Giga from *English Suite 3*	91
809/1	Prelude from *English Suite 4*	10
809/2	Allemande from *English Suite 4*	29
809/3	Courante from *English Suite 4*	44
809/4	Sarabande from *English Suite 4*	60
809/5	Menuet I from *English Suite 4*	79
809/7	Giga from *English Suite 4*	91
810/1	Prelude from *English Suite 5*	11
810/2	Allemande from *English Suite 5*	29
810/3	Courante from *English Suite 5*	44
810/4	Sarabande from *English Suite 5*	60
810/5	Passepied I from *English Suite 5*	82
810/7	Giga from *English Suite 5*	90
811/1	Prelude from *English Suite 6*	10–11
811/2	Allemande from *English Suite 6*	29
811/3	Courante from *English Suite 6*	44
811/4	Sarabande from *English Suite 6*	61
811/5	Sarabande Double from *English Suite 6*	62
811/8	Giga from *English Suite 6*	91
812–817	*French Suites*	5
812/1	Allemande from *French Suite 1*	30
812/2	Courante from *French Suite 1*	46
812/3	Sarabande from *French Suite 2*	65
812/4	Menuet I from *French Suite 1*	81
812/6	Gigue from *French Suite 1*	104
813/1	Allemande from *French Suite 2*	30
813/2	Corrente from *French Suite 2*	49
813/3	Sarabande from *French Suite 2*	63
813/4	Air from *French Suite 2*	84
813/5	Menuet I from *French Suite 2*	81
813/7	Gigue from *French Suite 2*	103
814/1	Allemande from *French Suite 3*	32
814/2	Courante from *French Suite 3*	48
814/3	Sarabande from *French Suite 3*	63
814/4	Anglaise from *French Suite 3*	84
814/7	Giga from *French Suite 3*	98
815/1	Allemande from *French Suite 4*	32
815/2	Corrente from *French Suite 4*	51
815/3	Sarabande from *French Suite 4*	65
815/4	Gavotte from *French Suite 4*	78
815/6	Air from *French Suite 4*	84
815/7	Giga from *French Suite 4*	98
816/1	Allemande from *French Suite 5*	30
816/2	Corrente from *French Suite 5*	52
816/3	Sarabande from *French Suite 5*	63
816/4	Gavotte from *French Suite 5*	77
816/5	Bourrée from *French Suite 5*	80
816/6	Loure from *French Suite 5*	88
816/7	Gigue from *French Suite 5*	101

100 ∞ THE DANCE SUITES

BWV Number	Title	Page(s)
817/1	Allemande from *French Suite 6*	30
817/2	Corrente from *French Suite 6*	52
817/3	Sarabande from *French Suite 6*	63
817/5	Polonaise from *French Suite 6*	88
811/7	Bourrée from *French Suite 6*	74
817/8	Giga from *French Suite 6*	98
825–830	*Keyboard Partitas*	5
825/1	Praeludium from *Keyboard Partita 1*	16
825/2	Allemande from *Keyboard Partita 1*	32
825/3	Corrente from *Keyboard Partita 1*	51
825/4	Sarabande from *Keyboard Partita 1*	69
825/7	Gigue from *Keyboard Partita 1*	101
826/1	Sinfonia from *Keyboard Partita 2*	21
826/2	Allemande from *Keyboard Partita 2*	33
826/3	Courante from *Keyboard Partita 2*	47
826/4	Sarabande from *Keyboard Partita 2*	67
826/5	Rondeaux from *Keyboard Partita 2*	88
826/6	Capriccio from *Keyboard Partita 2*	85
827/1	Fantasia from *Keyboard Partita 3*	17
827/2	Allemande from *Keyboard Partita 3*	31
827/3	Corrente from *Keyboard Partita 3*	52
827/4	Sarabande from *Keyboard Partita 3*	65
827/5	Burlesca from *Keyboard Partita 3*	87
827/6	Scherzo from *Keyboard Partita 3*	86
827/7	Giga from *Keyboard Partita 3*	100
828/1	Ouverture from *Keyboard Partita 4*	18
828/2	Allemande from *Keyboard Partita 4*	31
828/3	Courante from *Keyboard Partita 4*	46
828/4	Aria from *Keyboard Partita 4*	84
828/5	Sarabande from *Keyboard Partita 4*	64
828/7	Gigue from *Keyboard Partita 4*	101
829/1	Praeambulum from *Keyboard Partita 5*	13
829/2	Allemande from *Keyboard Partita 5*	31
829/3	Corrente from *Keyboard Partita 5*	50
829/4	Sarabande from *Keyboard Partita 5*	64
829/5	Tempo di Menuetta from *Keyboard Partita 5*	81
829/7	Giga from *Keyboard Partita 5*	98
830/1	Toccata from *Keyboard Partita 6*	16
830/2	Allemanda from *Keyboard Partita 6*	31–32
830/3	Corrente from *Keyboard Partita 6*	53
830/4	Sarabande from *Keyboard Partita 6*	69
830/5	Air from *Keyboard Partita 6*	84
830/6	Tempo di Gavotta from *Keyboard Partita 6*	78
830/7	Gigue from *Keyboard Partita 6*	104
831	*French Overture*	5
831/1	Overture from *French Overture*	19
831/2	Courante from *French Overture*	47
831/7	Sarabande from *French Overture*	64
831/10	Gigue from *French Overture*	102
831/11	Echo from *French Overture*	85
996	*Lute Suite 1*	5
996/1	Praeludio from *Lute Suite 1*	20
996/2	Allemande from *Lute Suite 1*	32
996/3	Courante from *Lute Suite 1*	46
996/4	Sarabande from *Lute Suite 1*	68
996/6	Giga from *Lute Suite 1*	99
997	*Lute Suite 2*	5
997/1	Preludio from *Lute Suite 2*	15
997/2	Fuga from *Lute Suite 2*	95
997/3	Sarabande from *Lute Suite 2*	66
997/4	Gigue from *Lute Suite 2*	103
997/5	Gigue Double from *Lute Suite 2*	103
1001–1006	*Violin Sonatas & Partitas*	5
1002/1	Allemanda from *Violin Partita 1*	35–36
1002/2	Allemanda Double from *Violin Partita 1*	36
1002/3	Corrente from *Violin Partita 1*	50
1002/4	Corrente Double from *Violin Partita 1*	50
1002/5	Sarabande from *Violin Partita 1*	67
1002/6	Sarabande Double from *Violin Partita 1*	68
1002/7	Tempo di Borea from *Violin Partita 1*	75

BWV Number	Title	Page(s)
1002/8	Tempo di Borea Double from *Violin Partita 1*	75
1004/1	Allemande from *Violin Partita 2*	31
1004/2	Corrente from *Violin Partita 2*	51
1004/3	Sarabande from *Violin Partita 2*	64
1004/4	Giga from *Violin Partita 2*	98
1004/5	Chaconne from *Violin Partita 2*	89
1006/1	Preludio from *Violin Partita 3*	13
1006/2	Loure from *Violin Partita 3*	87
1006/7	Giga from *Violin Partita 3*	98
1007–1012	*Cello Suites*	5
1007/1	Prelude from *Cello Suite 1*	13
1007/2	Allemande from *Cello Suite 1*	34
1007/3	Corrente from *Cello Suite 1*	53
1007/4	Sarabande from *Cello Suite 1*	66
1007/7	Giga from *Cello Suite 1*	99
1008/1	Prelude from *Cello Suite 2*	15
1008/2	Allemande from *Cello Suite 2*	31
1008/3	Corrente from *Cello Suite 2*	52
1008/4	Sarabande from *Cello Suite 2*	64
1008/7	Giga from *Cello Suite 2*	98
1009/1	Prelude from *Cello Suite 3*	13
1009/2	Allemande from *Cello Suite 3*	31
1009/3	Corrente from *Cello Suite 3*	49
1009/4	Sarabande from *Cello Suite 3*	64
1009/7	Giga from *Cello Suite 3*	99
1010/1	Prelude from *Cello Suite 4*	15
1010/2	Allemande from *Cello Suite 4*	34
1010/3	Corrente from *Cello Suite 4*	51
1010/4	Sarabande from *Cello Suite 4*	67
1010/7	Giga from *Cello Suite 4*	100
1011/1	Prelude from *Cello Suite 5*	19
1011/2	Allemande from *Cello Suite 5*	33
1011/3	Courante from *Cello Suite 5*	47
1011/4	Sarabande from *Cello Suite 5*	67
1011/7	Gigue from *Cello Suite 5*	103
1012/1	Prelude from *Cello Suite 6*	16
1012/2	Allemande from *Cello Suite 6*	37
1012/3	Corrente from *Cello Suite 6*	52
1012/4	Sarabande from *Cello Suite 6*	68
1012/7	Giga from *Cello Suite 6*	99
1066–1069	*Orchestral Suites*	4

www.ingramcontent.com/pod-product-compliance
Lightning Source LLC
Chambersburg PA
CBHW081311070526
44578CB00006B/835